*A Special Dedication*

*to*

*Terry and Carla*

*You were my cheerleaders, my technical advisors,*

*my proofreaders.*

*You were the veil, the thin barrier of support,*

*between my thoughts and my words on paper.*

*I Thank You!*

# LISTEN TO THE WHISPERS

### ... a walk in Widowhood

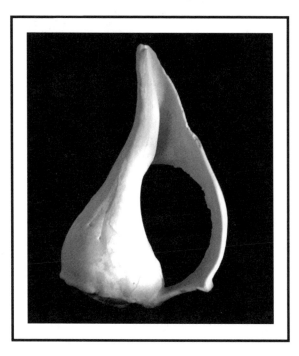

*by*

*Elizabeth P. Lane*

# LISTEN TO THE WHISPERS

## . . . a walk in Widowhood

Elizabeth P. Lane

In Loving Memory of Rudy Lane


Dedicated to Paige and Robyn
(the best daughters a Mother could ask for)

## ACKNOWLEDGEMENTS …

In grateful appreciation to family: Blair, Rhodes, Alle, David, Ann Garner, Lanie, Deni, Bill, Kyle, Jarad, A.W., Carrie, Beth, Duff, Whitney, Tyson, Kris, Don, Kelly, Tyler, Terry, Carla, Allyson, Mike, Debbie, Shane, Kate, Ben, Jeremy, Hilda, Vickie (in no special order)—your calls, cards, and letters are what kept me going – I love you!

In special appreciation to friends: Patti and Ann, Bob, Dee and Allen, Tim, Pat, Hall, my Trinity family, and too many others to name, but you certainly know who you are – I thank you!

And in Special Appreciation to my **Out-of-the-Box**: Barbara and Kaye (originals), Elaine, Cheryl, Betty B., Betty C., Janet, Glenda, Ann, Reba, Jean, Brenda, Susan, Anne, and Faye – Your journeys are what it's all about!

# CONTENTS

Forward .................................................................. 1

Death – The Worst Has Happened ................................ 3

Grief Has No Timetable ............................................. 5

Rushing to Stay Busy ................................................ 7

Emotions are Normal ................................................ 9

Grief Feels Tangible ................................................ 11

Life's New Chapter .................................................. 13

Healing – When? ..................................................... 17

Healing Takes Time .................................................. 19

OK to Cry ................................................................ 23

Depression .............................................................. 25

Anger – It's OK ....................................................... 27

Grief/Love .............................................................. 29

Listening to the Whispers ......................................... 31

The Question – How Are You? ................................... 33

Reading/Writing ...................................................... 35

Happiness??? .......................................................... 37

Self-Image .............................................................. 39

Low Energy ............................................................. 41

Melancholy ............................................................. 43

Empty Future...............................................................45

The Color of Grief.........................................................47

The "Now" Person .........................................................49

Lack of Self-Confidence ..................................................51

Reaching Out is Hard.....................................................55

The 'W' Word...............................................................57

Fear...........................................................................59

I Loved My Life............................................................61

Attention Span.............................................................63

Helping Others ............................................................67

Permission..................................................................69

This is Not Me..............................................................71

Second Chance at Life ....................................................73

Others are Grieving Too..................................................75

Where Do We Find God (Again)? ......................................79

What Can I Do?............................................................83

Joy ...........................................................................85

A New Beginning..........................................................87

And so . . ...................................................................89

Notes ........................................................................91

Footsteps ...................................................................95

# FORWARD

*Your life stops right there. Just stops. And when it starts up again, it's different. It's never what it was before that moment. Never.*
—— Nora Roberts (Novel - Black Rose)

For those of you who have not experienced this chapter in your life, this is the story no one ever tells you: the absolute loneliness, the fear of the unknown, the monumental task of building a new You, much less a new life.

For those of you who are Fellow Travelers, this is a book of Hope. I want you to know you are not alone, and I want you to know you are not crazy. You have memory lapses; you talk to your loved one; you do not have the energy to face another day, much less to deal with another legal request or even to answer the phone. It's OK.

For a long time I truly believed life does not get better after the death of your loved one, or even easier; I believed it just became different as you filled the void with life of a different concept. Through time, I have found I was wrong. With time, you adjust, and perhaps that is what makes life easier. As time passes, you become more and more thankful for the moments, weeks, months, years, you shared with your loved one.

You realize you are grateful for the shared impact you both had on each other's life. It becomes a love story of a different dimension, one that can never be taken from you. Treasure the memories, for they are what sustain you over the rough spots of the future.

> *Life changes in an instant.*
> *The ordinary instant.*
>
> —— Joan Didion

You will rebuild yourself, and you will rebuild your life. You don't have a choice. Your new life will be what **YOU** make it. Make it the best that you can be.

Make it so in memory of your loved one. What else would they expect?

*Thanks be to God, and Listen to the Whispers . . .*

# DEATH – THE WORST HAS HAPPENED

I had heard my sister-in-law, Debbie, a Baptist minister's wife, say many times after some happening, "It's not the worst thing that can happen." Finally, after a really deep finger cut and many stitches, I commented on the pain and near tragic experience. Yes, she voiced this thought once again. I suddenly said, Well, Debbie, what *is* the WORST thing that can happen?

I still remember the scene. We were in the kitchen preparing a Holiday dinner. She turned slowly and just stared at me. She then said very quietly, "Death, Beth. Death is the worst thing that can happen."

I was stunned. Of course. How could I not know? I am there.

Trust me, until you have experienced the death of your spouse, your soul mate, your child, someone really close, you do not fully comprehend or truly understand or even appreciate that statement.

You are suddenly thrown into a new life, one you did not ask for and one you did not want. You are now part of a 'different' group of people. Your friends, and sometimes your family, do not know what to do with you. You are different now, and they do not know how to deal with that difference. That's OK. You don't know how to deal with you either. Each day is a new experience, one you don't even want to face. But you do.

You don't have a choice.

This book is about this new US.

3

*The 'ripple effect' – the way selfless acts can have an impact on more than those who are served directly, by influencing those who simply observe.*

(Tyler & Day by Day)

The day before I read this, my grandson, Tyler, had given me encouragement saying if this book only helped one person, the ripple effect would create the helping of many.

# GRIEF HAS NO TIMETABLE

I have always believed there was no timetable for grief. A friend said to me she had been told you don't have the right to grieve after a year. Without thinking, I replied, "Bulls...!" I realized again it was time for me to write this book. If I have learned one thing, it is DO NOT compare and DO NOT judge. Your grief is your own, no one else's. And no one has the right to tell you to move on. I have also learned that the grief process cannot and should not be hurried.

Joan Didion wrote in her book, *A Year of Magical Thinking:* "Grief turns out to be a place none of us know until we reach it." Only you know.

Because I tell you there is no timetable does not mean that you cannot move on with your life. We do – we have to. I have a friend who travels and entertains on a regular basis, but she confided in me she knew she would grieve the rest of her life. Another friend did most of her grieving while her ailing husband was alive. Her grief has been a long and strenuous path .

The evidence of what I knew I read in an article in the magazine 'O' – December 2006 – written by the news reporter, Lynn Sherr. She had spent six years knowing her husband was dying and several more years trying to find closure. Her breakthrough came in a story she was doing for 20/20 on the agony of loss. Interviewing Jimmie Holland, a pioneering psychiatrist at New York's Memorial Sloan-Kettering Cancer Center, Dr. Holland said the medical profession had been putting people into stages for years and encouraging a certain amount of time to grieve and then move on. Her words to Lynn were, "Well, wrong! You can't do this to people. Your pattern of grief is as unique as your pattern of love." She freed Lynn to mourn and to know it was not self-indulgence. It was a wonderful two page article I sent to my Out-of-the-Box Group. Lynn ended saying she had finally learned to live without her husband, but not to forget him, and "to honor the memory of what was, while functioning in the world that is."

Isn't this what we all want and strive toward? The timetable is yours, and don't let anyone tell you otherwise. REMEMBER AGAIN: Do Not Judge; Do Not Compare.


*Have patience with all things, but chiefly have patience with yourself.*

—— Saint Francis DeSales

# Rushing to Stay Busy is Normal

After the initial time, which I call The Peace Period, I went through a period of all-consuming busyness, rushing constantly to fill the hours. My daughter, Paige, had just started a new business. I volunteered to help, so I would not have to think. I only went to my own office as I needed to or had to. My husband's workshop was there also; it was too much of a reminder. On weekends I rushed to grandchildren's ballgames. I worked so hard at staying busy and on the go that my youngest daughter, Robyn, became worried about my health and well being. At that time she was a Personal Trainer for several older ladies who had been widows for years. She expressed her concern to one of her clients who only smiled and said,"It's a phase, Robyn. This too shall pass." And it did.

I still believe the key to taking steps forward is in staying busy. But I no longer have to fill every minute and rush from one thing to the next. I can sit with silence and just 'be.'

*Do not fear mistakes. There are none.*

—— Miles Davis

8

## EMOTIONS ARE NORMAL

My friend, Pat, in North Carolina, moved to Georgia at the time of her first anniversary. She had been dealing with health issues for herself and her daughter during this first year; she had put her grief on a shelf. On this first anniversary, she related experiencing all five elements of grief in one horrible day. She said she had read these were commonly shared emotions for the grief process, which she had not yet encountered.

Denial

Guilt

Anger

Grief

Acceptance

She was referring to the most commonly known elements experienced by those who lose a loved one. Please know that this in no way means you have to experience all five.

When she first related these to me, I thought I had escaped two: Guilt and Anger. I know this is true of anger, because my husband, Rudy, had such a good attitude of acceptance – how could I have less? Faith is my key. I thought GUILT was escaped until later I realized that all the first basketball games I would sit, with tears in my eyes, feeling HE should be there instead of me. In my heart I know he was there, just in another dimension.

Listen to the Whispers . . .

*Do Not Judge*
*Do Not Compare*
*Do Something for Someone Else*

—— epl

## GRIEF FEELS TANGIBLE

Grief feels tangible in the early stages. It engulfs us as a cloud. We walk in its haze. We feel it and taste it, as it touches us in the deepest parts of our soul. Time lifts the cloud; but, as we all know, fog can roll back over us at the most unexpected times.

Martha Whitmore Hickman wrote these words:
*" I will watch for other travelers on the way who may need my help, as I need theirs."*

This is why I am writing this book. I want others to hear and know that this grief and mourning is a time in which things as we knew them are suspended. What we feel and experience is 'normal' to each of us. As Joan Didion wrote in her book, *The Year of Magical Thinking*, "we are not "crazy" as in the mental and medical definition or sense. We have gone through a major shock. We are affected in all parts of our body. This means our mind as well as our heart. We do not think straight; it is hard to make decisions; our attention span is shorter. This is OK; we are not 'crazy.' We are lethargic; some days it is hard to even function. This is OK; again, we are not 'crazy.' We talk to our loved one; some of us even feel anger. It is normal; we are not crazy."
This too shall pass.

11

*In the end, the object of what I write is not so much that people will know me and my stories so much as it is that they will know their own stories and then perhaps themselves a little better.*

—— Robert Benton (author)

## LIFE'S NEW CHAPTER

If you are reading this, the chances are you are in a new chapter of your life. You may have been thrown in as I was, or the approach may have been slowly occurring for a terrible and aching period of time. Regardless, you did not choose this chapter; you do not want it. The bottom line is – we have to live it. How do we get to the next chapter? Is there a next chapter? How do we become whole again?

Please let me emphasize - I do not write this to set an example. I do not write this to be a mentor. Again, I write this as a fellow traveler and, perhaps, friend. I write this to say what you are experiencing is normal; it is OK. It is OK to be confused. It is OK to hurt physically and emotionally. It is OK to cry. You are not "crazy."

You are unique. This chapter of your life is yours. The slate is clean for you, and you write the words. You LIVE the words. Sometimes the words stack, day upon day, like pancakes. Some days the words fall like blocks. And, believe it or not, some days the words are brief rays of sunshine peaking through the clouds.

In my searching for relief and understanding, I read many books. One of these described this period as a black hole that you have to walk into in order to get through. Perhaps you feel you were thrown into this darkness, and you see no light.

REMEMBER THIS: You cannot rush this chapter. You have no choice; you have to live it. Some people feel they can rush this, but it always seems to come back and haunt them at a later date.

This was not intended to be a religious book; however, I will tell you this. I could not have made this walk without my faith. I know God carried me through the 'worst.' I vividly remember experiencing the wonderful calmness that was like a protective veil engulfing me throughout the time of the funeral and continuing for a time afterwards. One of my daughters even commented on my patience with the grandchildren. I also remember vividly losing this calmness. The grandchildren had spent the night, and we were getting ready for church. I lost my cool when they weren't getting ready and were still playing. I suddenly realized the "peace" was gone. Reality had set in.

I wanted the 'peace' back, but I could not retrieve it. New steps were in front of me, and there was no direction to go but forward.

Please remember that the experiences I relate do not mean the same ones will or should occur with you. Again, REMEMBER: Your story is unique to you, and it should be. I only relate mine to stress the words again – It's OK. Hopefully, and this is definitely the intention, you will find some comfort in the words of a fellow traveler.

*Woman must come of age by herself – she must find her true center alone. If one is out of touch with oneself, then one cannot touch others.*

—— Anne Morrow Lindbergh

## Healing – When?

Sometime in the first year after my husband's death, I attended a church dinner called Ladies' Night Out. Several widows hovered around me, in concerned love. One assured me it does get better, in time. Another one spoke up and said, "When? I still relive the night he died, over and over."

Isn't this what we all feel at times? As I have stated, I used to feel: "It doesn't get better; life becomes different as we rebuild it. And some call 'this' better." While this is true, I was also wrong. Time works curiously and slowly while we are not even aware.

Margaret Hickman Whitmore wrote:

*We will not always be at this point of Altered Reality. We will, in time, incorporate our loss into our lives so that it is part of the daily background of living.*

Many of you are still at a stage where you cannot imagine this part of your grief being part of your background. Trust me. It will happen.

This doesn't mean I do not still have times that my insides ache for my love and our life together. Trust me. The bursts of depression happen less frequently and are shorter in time. The love is still there, just on a different level.

REMEMBER THIS: *We must be willing to get rid of the life we've planned, so as to have the life that is waiting for us.*

—— Joseph Campbell.

This quote has been the hardest of all for me. I feel your incompleteness; I feel your aloneness.

Take my words in, and know you are not alone.

*When one door closes another door opens; but we so often look so long and so regretfully upon the closed door, that we do not see the ones which open for us.*

—— Alexander Graham Bell

## HEALING TAKES TIME

As part of my "healing" I initiated an **Out-Of-The-Box** dinner group. I started with two, to whom I had been sending notes of encouragement. I wanted to start cooking again, even if it was once a month. Cooking had been a joy my husband and I shared, but I did not find joy in cooking for one. (Are you relating?) I decided to remodel my kitchen, cosmetically, to make it my own and perhaps add credence to my new **Out-of-the-Box** decision. My husband was a wonderful cook, and we shared many happy hours there cooking together. (Do you see the pattern?) I was searching for joy.

This has become a wonderful group of new friends. I send out invitations for a mostly monthly dinner. I follow up with recipes used that night, as well as words of encouragement. We now have 18. We did not solicit new people – they appeared. We don't have an agenda. We just have something to look forward to, with fellow travelers. We are each stepping-out-of-the-box in attending, because, number one – it's an effort and, number two – we did not know each other very well and sometimes not at all. If we feel like crying, or talking about what we are going through, it is OK; because we are fellow travelers. The Purpose is to reach out and help someone . The result is to also help ourselves.

We are each, myself included, encouraged to take a risk and step out of our comfort zone. Again, I stress not comparing. Just as we all hurt differently, we all take steps differently. What is a small risk to one person may be a hugh risk to another. What may have been quite normal in your 'other' life may now seem monumental. I encourage my out-of-the-box friends to "step out" at least once during the month. The victory is theirs. They only have to share it if they so desire. One of the ladies shared early on buying fresh flowers just for herself.

Other suggestions for Stepping-Out-Of-Your Box may be:

- Going to a restaurant alone
- Having a dinner party as a single
- Renting a video for yourself (it's amazing how little things are suddenly daunting)
- Going to the movie alone
- Buying a piece of art – just for yourself
- Having a massage – why not?
- Taking a trip alone or with acquaintances (not necessarily close friends)

- Changing the way you dress
- Changing hair style or color
- Read a book uncharacteristic for you (you might like it!)
- Listen to different music
- Volunteer
- Take art lessons

Some or all of these probably have been a normal part of your 'other' life; now they may seem huge. Set a goal for yourself – *your* goal – STEP OUT at least once a month too. You will be amazed at what each small victory will do for your self-esteem. Begin to care about yourself.

*Healing begins with caring.*

—— Bill Moyer

# OK TO CRY

It is acceptable and perfectly normal to cry. Martha Whitmore Hickman wrote:

*No more apologies. My tears are my healing. Perhaps, too, my tears will give others permission to cry when they feel the need.*

This is so true. Record it in your heart.

Grief is non-denominational. Each person is unique; therefore, their grief is as unique as yours to you.

In my readings, I found this wonderful and revealing anonymous quote:

*If someone cries in front of me, I consider it a gift.*

I now fully understand and feel the magnitude of that 'gift.'

As time passes and we begin to become a whole person again (and we will), we realize the hurt is still there, just as the love is still there, and will always be; but it is becoming a part of our 'inner' self. Perhaps this is what some call "getting better."

*We feel we are alone in our strivings but we are not. Pain makes us reach out; and when we do, we connect and realize that others, too, have traveled along the same path. This is how we grow.*

—— Alexandra Stoddard

## DEPRESSION

I never thought depression was in my life, even after my husband died. I now realize it is in everyone's life. We just do not always recognize it for what it is.

When I feel lost, as I have often felt since my husband's death, I am in a stage of depression. When I am sad, it is a form of depression.

Some time after my husband's death, I was asked by my priest to attend a Lenten Study. One session would be on grief and depression. I did not feel I needed this particular segment, but he obviously saw or knew something I did not. I simply joined the group because he had called and asked me. During the particular week we touched on grief, we each had to take a private quiz, answering Yes or No to perhaps 20 questions. I was shocked to find I could answer Yes to *all* but the two regarding thoughts of suicide. I was depressed and did not even know it!

This was my first recognition of depression of the heart and soul. I learned a valuable lesson – depression does not have to mean you take to your bed, or that you become recluse, or that you need medication and/or counseling. Depression can take many forms and feelings. It can be, and is often, simply a deep sadness within, which can sometimes easily be hidden from others.

I am so thankful I was asked to attend that Study Group. I can, hopefully, now recognize and better respond to these deep, Normal, feelings in myself and others.

REMEMBER ALSO THIS: Do not judge others because they are not responding or acting as you feel they should or as you did. Do not judge others because they are more publicly demonstrative than you. Again, we are all unique in our grief.

*When you "least" feel like it, do something for someone else.*
—— Dana Reeve (Christopher Reeve's wife)

# ANGER – IT'S OK

I have read time and again that many people go through an angry stage. This is natural and part of grieving. It is not right or wrong whether or not you experience this stage.

Many of us go through constant analyzing of our feelings. I fully know and appreciate the reason I personally did not go through this stage. One of the times my husband was hospitalized with pneumonia, our priest, Tim Murphy, came to the hospital. It was early on in my husband's illness, and he had refused to share his situation unless someone specifically asked. He wanted no pity; and above all, he wanted to live a normal life. In Tim's special manner, and knowing my husband, he said, "OK, Rudy, I am just going to ask – what's wrong with you?" My husband explained he had a rare blood disease, which in layman's terms was called pre-leukemia. After he had finished explaining, Tim asked him how was his relationship with God. Rudy said, "What do you mean?" Tim wanted to know if he was angry with God because he had this disease. Rudy answered, no, he wasn't angry; why should 'he' be exempt from getting this disease; why should 'he' think he was so special as to be excluded from illness.

I have never forgotten this message. If Rudy wasn't angry, how could I be? I am truly thankful to have had this man as my husband for

19 years. It wasn't long enough, but is it ever long enough? I am simply grateful for the time we shared.

Regardless of 'my' situation, I firmly believe anger is normal. Sometimes the anger is at God. Believe me, He understands. Sometimes the anger is at our loved one for leaving us, not taking better care of themselves, or sometimes, all of the above. It doesn't have to be logical to others, or even to ourselves. It is 'our' grief, and it is OK.

The key is not to let this anger consume you. If you do, you may lose your wonderful memories. Again, the memories are what sustain us.

When you feel the anger coming on, vent it if you can (hopefully without hurting someone else). Cry if you feel like it. Then put a lid back on the can of emotions, and conjure up a good memory. Try to laugh. Keep trying this until you reach a point where you can forgive. Forgive yourself, forgive your loved one, forgive God.

If you cannot seem to get through this anger, seek professional help. Sometimes this is the only and best recourse. It's OK.

REMEMBER THIS: Keep pulling up the good memories. Try to laugh.

*A day without laughter is like a day without sunshine.*

—— Rudy Lane

## GRIEF/LOVE

Along with the initial intensity of grief is an enormous degree of love for the one we have lost. Sometimes the two are so intertwined that, as we cling to this intensified love, we also cling to the grief. But just as the strength of true love matures in a marriage and becomes better and has flashes of intensities, we recognize we could not live at that heightened level all the time. As we recognize that the maturing of love is good, we come to also know this is what happens in the normal course of grief. This is what we want, a maturing of the grief/love. We also could not bear this intensity of grief/love for a lifetime.

The key, as I see it, is not to 'work' at 'getting rid of' the grief, for grief needs and demands its own time. Nor should we try to hold on to this intensity of the love. Love does not leave us. It matures with us, as it should.

REMEMBER THIS: Treasure the memories – keeping the good and discarding the not so good.

*Bereavement of married love is but one of its regular phases – like the honeymoon. What we want is to live our marriage well and faithfully through that phase (bereavement), too.*

—— C.S. Lewis – *A Grief Observed*

## LISTENING TO THE WHISPERS

We Listen to the Whispers, because we want to believe our loved one is still there. In this new realm of awareness, we become more attuned; because we don't want to lose this bond.

I had always been afraid of death. I am no longer. I truly know my loved one is there and will be when my time comes. It was hard for me to "let go" of needing his presence. He finally came to me through a friend in a vision and said, "I am home." I experienced a great sadness and cried. I realized I was crying for myself. I had 'hung on' too long. He knew this before I did. He knew before I did that I would be OK and that it was time. This experience does not happen to everyone. But I sincerely believe it happened for me. He knew how much I still needed him, and he was there as long as he could be. Again, this does not happen to everyone.

REMEMBER: Do not compare.

*I wonder. If, as I can't help suspecting, the dead also feel the pains of separation (this may be part of their purgatorial sufferings), then for both lovers, bereavement is a universal and integral part of our experience of love.*

—— C.S. Lewis

# THE QUESTION – HOW ARE YOU?

THE question seems to always be there. Family and friends are concerned, and they ask – How are you? Your answer is always the same – I'm fine; I'm OK; good days and bad days – routine question; routine answers.

My husband used to say when people ask how are you or how is your day, they did not expect an answer. He sometimes would play a game and say with a smile (the important part) - terrible, just lost my dog, etc. etc. The person would not even hear the answer; they just saw the smile and keep going.

Then someone "really" looks into your eyes and asks softly, " How ARE you?"

Sometimes you burst into tears. It is so hard to be honest, and it is so hard to really say, "I don't know. It's all new; one step at a time." It's the same world to everyone else. WE are the ones who are different. WE are the ones building a new life. WE are the ones with tender feelings. Our friends and family have gone back to their lives, as they should. WE are the ones looking at everything through new eyes and feeling our way across our scarred battlefield of a life. For it IS a battle to get up every morning and face the world alone when only 'yesterday' we were so happy.

So how do you answer those who really do care and honestly want to know? With simple honesty and a quiet resolve – I may not always know, but I'm working on it.

*Sorrow is not a state, but a process.*

—— C.S. Lewis

## READING/WRITING

As is the case with many, several people gave me books after my husband died. Although I eventually read them all, the one which helped the most was *Healing After Loss*, by Martha Whitmore Hickman. It was more like a Day-by-Day, short and within my limited attention span at that time. Although I have kept my original, given by my good friend, Adrienne Ford, who had lost a son, I have purchased many copies for new widows. It speaks.

You must decide what is best for you. Reading may be your source of help or writing in a journal, or both. There is no right or wrong.

I had been told that writing in a journal was helpful. I am a 'tight' person who does not share easily. In the beginning I could not 'share' on paper, even with myself. I have another friend, who 'writes' to her deceased spouse every night. You must do what helps you.

As time passed, and I had read so few books which really helped me, I began to see that "I" might be a helper to others. I wrote first on March 21, 2004, three days after what would have been my husband's birthday. It had been one year and six months. It is now five years later. It has helped me to express my feelings. If you feel so led, perhaps you will be able to start sooner than I. No one has to read what you write. At the appropriate time, you can burn or discard the pages.

The choice is always yours.

As Martha Whitmore Hickman said, "It may help you sort things out, and you will be free to move on into the next moments of your life."

I have taken her words to heart. (I have read her book three complete times and highlighted areas more than this.) Perhaps after writing this book, not only may it help someone else, perhaps I will better be able to move on to the next chapter of my life.

*Our inner condition, rather than our outer circumstances, is what truly defines us.*

—— Roger Housden

# HAPPINESS ???

C.S. Lewis wrote: *No one ever told me about the laziness of grief, the loathing of even the slightest effort; feeling – what does it even matter now? (writing, reading, even shaving). And: Grief feels like fear and, more strictly, suspense – waiting, provisional – life doesn't seem worth starting anything. Up until this time I had too little time; now there is nothing but time – empty.* (paraphrased)

Apathy is the norm. What is happiness, but a lost feeling.

Happiness is no longer what it once was. Regardless, we still have the ability to choose happiness, perhaps not in the beginning, but at some point. It is up to each of us to bring light into our own lives again.

If you need, reread what I have just said, again and again if need be. You may be saying – You don't understand; this is impossible.

Believe me. I understand. My husband was my best friend, and he was quite simply my sun. He was my crucial light for laughter and happiness. I do know where you are.

As we try to do even simple things, they simply just are not as much fun. I know. But we have to keep trying and cheering each other on. That's right. We now have a responsibility to others who have experienced the 'worst' as we have. We are in a sisterhood/brotherhood all our own and certainly not our choosing. My way, as yours, is

37

tentative, but yielding light, none the less, through memories, warmth of home, family, and friends, old and new.

REMEMBER THIS: "It's OK" is giving yourself permission to experience grief your way. Well meaning friends and family tell you 'they are in a better place' and 'you wouldn't want them to suffer' and 'you are being selfish' or, even worse, perhaps they avoid you altogether. Try not to take offense. They have never been in the place you are. Remember you were once in their shoes. You did not know what to say then either.

Try to take pleasure in the small things. I invite you to try, by Stepping Out-of-Your-Box. As Mick Jaggar sings,

> *You can't always get what you want;*
> *But if you try sometime,*
> *You just might find,*
> *You get what you need.*

*Even, and perhaps especially, at moments of great sadness, we need to laugh.*

—— *Zen Paths to Laughter*

## Self Image

In this vulnerable new chapter of our lives, some of us may realize we don't like ourselves right now. Of course we don't. We've lost one half of our person. We feel deformed. But it is really our life we don't like. We want the old one back. We are insecure, as we search for our new self.

I know one woman who redid her whole house. Her daughter said – I don't know why she's doing this. I 'now' know. It was part of searching for her new identity. Some people move, even to a new town. It may appear to others to be running away. It is really part of the search.

For me, it has been my hair. I know this appears silly, but it has been very real to me. (Reminder: if you have a bad hair day, you have a bad start on your day. We all know that.) For me, my illogical part of the brain kicked into gear big time about my hair. Logically, I realize my husband was no longer here to tell me I was beautiful (of course, I'm not beautiful, but in his eyes, I was). Therefore, suddenly my hair became super important. I kept trying new styles and shades. Finally one of my daughters suggested I try someone in another town who appraised you and did it his way. It's getting better.

Thanks be to God for daughters. They have helped me with this illogical problem. They now are my re-enforcers. Of course, it is not the same; but it helps bring in the reality. They have assumed this special role which has extended into my wardrobe. All my life I have favored blacks and browns. They have brought color into my clothes. I have accepted this 'help', with mostly good nature. I keep reminding myself, it is part of my Stepping Out-Of-My Box, this new me.

They are also my strongest supporters. They are there to help me with the self-image inside as well as out. Our fragile selves need support from family and friends.

**Paige**: You have to find that place within where you are comfortable. (I'm still working on this.)

**Robyn**: If you question yourself, you damage the memories you have. (So True)

*"Some things happen to us from which we never recover, and they disrupt the normalcy of our lives. We must forget 'the old standard' and accept a "new normal."*

—— Don Piper

## LOW ENERGY

Low energy is normal. Sometimes it is so bad, we see a doctor to find out if something is physically wrong. I went through two and a half years with first no energy and then very low energy, with no real purpose or direction. In reflecting on this late one night with my brother, Terry, he gave me this insight:

"Beth, you and Rudy had such strong energy 'together.' With his death, you lost half of that energy. It takes time to rebuild it."

We all need to be reminded that we are human. My brother was right. This is part of making the new me.

Margaret Whitmore Hickman wrote:

*I will live through these days the best I can; trusting that in time my spontaneity and energy will return.*

Grief is a very private existence. We grow up hearing and saying: *Blessed are Those Who Mourn.* Of course, it is different when it happens to oneself. REMEMBER THIS: What you see on the exterior may not be what is on the inside. This is part of the Do Not Compare; Do Not Judge.

*Sometimes the "best I can" is just to endure.*

—— Don Piper

## MELANCHOLY

I first read of melancholy in relation to what I was experiencing in Martha Whitmore Hickman's *Healing After Loss*, 'a kind of low-key sadness.' I thought to myself: Melancholy — yes — perfect word, perfect word. Isn't this what fills our total self after the intense grief begins to slowly drift away? Faced with stark white reality, our life goes into the foggy gray zone of melancholy. And, as with fog, this feeling of sadness is sometimes extremely dense and sometimes patchy and occasionally lifts enough for rays of sunshine to peak through. Melancholy is the perfect word for this chapter of our lives. It is a blanket engulfing us in lethargy and depression during the times of dense fog and simple sadness, during the patches of fog.

We have to work on walking, with baby steps, hands outstretched, finding our way out. Some days, or parts of days, are more successful than others. Staying busy; getting a 'jobette,' as my friend Charlotte once said; volunteering; doing something for someone else helps. WE have to make it happen, the pulling ourselves out of the fog.

By the same token, if you simply cannot make it through this fog of melancholy alone, by all means, seek professional help, and quickly. REMEMBER THIS: There are certain times in our lives when we all need help. It's OK. This is not a bad thing. What would be tragic would be not getting the help needed so we can move on to the next chapter.

*You have to learn to 'let' people help you. It is their way of showing their love and concern. It is their gift.*

—— epl

## EMPTY FUTURE

Lisa Gardner used this poignant quote in her novel *Gone*:

*It was not the past that broke you. It was the empty future, the endless string of days filled with none of the people who mattered most.*

Once you've been in this empty void, you know and feel the gray confusion of this time. And it is a color – gray. We each have to work our own way out of this cold, damp, and dismal place. We have to learn to fill this 'empty future' day by day. But we each have to do it our own way.

What works for me (most of the time) is not to dwell on the vast void of the future and to keep busy in the present, no longer at a frantic pace, but a calm, steady busy.

Nora Roberts said in her novel, *Divided in Death:* "Life is never as long as you want it to be."

We now all know and live the stark truth of that statement.

I wish I could give you a magic answer. I wish I could say – this amount of time and it will be over. I am only a fellow traveler. I do not and cannot write this to tell you what to do or not to do. I am simply reaching out to you to say – what you are experiencing is normal; you are not crazy.

This is your time.

REMEMBER THIS:

*No one can go through this for you.*

Be kind to yourself.

Forgive yourself for not being the perfect wife or mother. (no one is)

Give yourself permission to grieve and mourn for as long as YOU need.

We now tend to equate happenings in our life in terms of 'before' and 'after.' This is natural. After all, we are no longer the same person we were 'before.' Our future will be what we make it.

Jerry Sittser in *A Grace Disguised* wrote:

*It is not, therefore, the 'experience' of loss that becomes the defining moment of our lives . . . it is how we 'respond' to loss that matters. That response will largely determine the quality, the direction, and the impact of our lives.*

I'm still working on this one.

*When infinite longing comes, take a walk, write a poem, call a friend.*

—— Perry E. Gresham - *With Wings As Eagles*

# THE COLOR OF GRIEF

At a time of grief, you do not want to 'think,' and, yet, all you do is think. You relive, over and over, the actual period of dying, rethinking all possibilities, logical and illogical.

For me, the color of grief is gray. When I think about this, I realize my brother, Terry, told me I was going through a "gray" period in my life; because, as an avid collector of art, I have suddenly been drawn to, rearranged for, and added to my collection – grays, browns, and blacks. I looked around me and suddenly see this is true. I have added black and white photos, framed and matted in grays and blacks, to my walls. Two central pictures purchased in memory of my husband (a ritual started with my parents) are in dark, somber hues. One now hangs above my fireplace. It has replaced three vivid paintings of English countryside framed in white. The second one is beside my bed – also total grays. It is the first and last vision I see each day. But I find this soothing. I have added a wall of old etchings, pens and inks, dark watercolors, above my bed – a European look, but in soothing dark tones. As I would normally do, I purchased a piece of art on a trip to Charleston with friends. It spoke to me from a large park of art – grays and browns and blacks – but now with a touch of blue. Perhaps my brother is truly insightful. My Gray Period may be inspired by my grief. But, never the less, it comforts me. And, it may be as a mist of warming fog, but it is ME for now.

Once again, my point is – this is YOUR time. You are the one traveling through the 'black hole.'

Be kind to yourself. There is no easy way through grief, no way to speed up the process. You just have to live it.

*It's a small fraternity, and none of us joined by choice.*

—— epl

## THE 'NOW' PERSON

We are no longer a 'we.' How do we discover who we are now? I
wish there was an easy answer. Do this; do that; follow this plan and it
will work out. It just does not happen that way. Just as we are all unique,
we all must walk our own path through the maze of grief and beyond,
with trials and errors. It's OK. No one is perfect.

How do we ease this pain of loss as we are trying to find our way in
this new world? We don't. It's real. I do know it is a constant search. I
do know I have a lot of questions I did not have before, questions about
life's purpose, life hereafter, where the soul of the loved one physically is
– with us unseen ? – where is heaven really, and on and on. I also know
I would not have been able to bear any of this without God's help. Even
though I have questions, I do not question the existence of God. I 'know'
He has carried me when I could not walk.

Sometimes you need to voice how you feel with family or friends.
They love you, but they cannot read your mind. They also may not be as
patient as you would like or expect. You have to lead the way for them to
help or listen. Just say – I need to talk about what's going on with me.

Each of us is "coming of age" in this new chapter. We have to do
it by ourselves. We alone must find our true center. One has to come to
terms with oneself, not only in a new stage of life, but in a new role –
living for one's self and no longer a 'we.'

*Grief: The raindrops of sadness; the tears of the soul.*

———— epl

# LACK OF SELF-CONFIDENCE

Just as we suddenly feel we have lost our identity and, with it, our self-confidence, we are very vulnerable and fragile. Our feelings are raw. We no longer feel confident doing things we have always done. We feel on display, the object of talk or pity. We are suddenly self-conscious.

How do we regain that control of our lives; how do we regain that self-confidence we always took for granted? Again, there is no easy answer. We have to work on it. One of the ways is stepping out of our box and doing things we don't really want to or have the energy to. We do it by helping someone else, even anonymously. Each time we do, we can be proud of ourselves. We can even 'reward' ourselves.

Alexandra Stoddard wrote: *Trust our inner consciousness. Self-awareness increases our self-confidence.*

Part of this regaining of self-confidence is, naturally, finding out – who am I now? We walk a path all our own to redefine or even reinvent this person who is ME.

Oprah wrote:

*What is your purpose, what is your calling? What I know for sure is, if you ask the question, the answer will come. You have to be willing to listen for the answer. You have to get still enough to learn it and hear it and pay attention, to be fully conscious enough to see not just with your eyes but through them to the truth of who you are and what you can be.*

A new friend of mine who has been a widow for some years, suggested that I think about things I might have always wanted to do but had been placed aside because it did not interest my spouse or because I had been mother and caretaker of family life. For some of us, it is a novel idea to suddenly put our wants and desires first. This is part of the healing.

Martha Whitmore Hickman wrote that coming into this personal wakefulness through grief is like giving birth with difficulty. She further encourages attention to our own needs, our state of mind through reading, rest, a willingness to be vulnerable again, counseling if needed, prayer and/or meditation, and even participation in a healing community. She adds: What we can be sure of is that we will be different.

C.S. Lewis wrote about feeling dazed, almost as if having a concussion. He expounded further by saying his life felt like it was in suspense, with thoughts, feelings, and actions that had once been directed toward the loved one and now the target is gone.

We can all choose adjectives that described that initial time, or even now. One of mine would be automatic pilot. But, at some point, we have to take the instruments off automatic. Coming back into the real world increases the pain and awareness, but it is the only way to heal and even grow. But I cannot stress strongly enough, it must be in your own time, not someone else's.

This is YOUR grief; only you know when to take the next step.

*"I don't know how to exist in a world where my Dad isn't."*
—— The Character 'George' in *Grey's Anatomy*

## Reaching Out is Hard

Taking that step to reach out when you need to talk is monumental. A new friend who was a widow of two and a half months called to ask me to go to dinner. She probably did not know how big a step this was. I did. Even though we had talked and visited and communicated in cards, I knew in my heart what courage it took for her to call and ask me to meet her for dinner. She was at a point of intense emotions of grief and anger. However, she was one of the fortunate ones who realized she needed help and reached out. She reached out to her doctor for her depression, and she reached out to a grief counselor. I felt honored she had also reach out to me. This was good.

This is a new role for all of us. Believe me, at some point you will be in a position or will be asked to help someone else. You will do it without thinking, and it will help you. It appears that God brings people into our lives who need us, giving us the opportunity to touch their lives as someone else has touched ours.

*One of the deep secrets of life is that all that is really worth doing is what we do for others.*

—— Lewis Caroll

## THE 'W' WORD

Especially in the beginning, we all despise the 'W' word. We still feel we are a wife, and we don't want that to change, even though it has. But, as time eases the intensity of grief, it also eases the intensity of feeling of the 'W' word. A widow is not something we want to be, and it is not something we would have chosen. It has been thrust upon you, and we are not prepared. For a long time we still feel married, so how can we accept being a Widow? I can only tell you Time and Grace eases us through this period.

I have learned to cope with the "W' word. I no longer feel it is a large black capital letter, forged on my body for all to see, as in the story of the *Scarlett Letter*. I try to remember it is an honored position in the eyes of God, honored 'W's'– Widow as well as Wife.

*You just need to get past this . . . Stop going over the way things used to be. Discover what I have now and build on it.*

—— Don Piper

# FEAR

I see and hear fears in each of us. Fear is one of the demons we fight – fear of the unknown, fear of being alone, fear of being taken advantage of, fear of finances, fear of fear itself, and on and on.

*A Day by Day* author wrote: *Years ago a wise counselor spoke of a frightened little boy who walked by my side warning me of every possible pitfall and danger, making me anxious and fretful. Rather than kick or escape or deny him, she suggested my task was to take him by the hand, listen to his warnings, and tell him that together we are going to make it.*

And we are. REMEMBER THIS: We ALL have our fears. Although they are unique unto our person and situation, they are also so similar because of our circumstances.

Fears are not always of our circumstances either. Sometimes it is fear of not remembering our loved one as we did or fear of losing mental contact with our lost one. Martha Whitmore Hickman wrote: *"Sometimes we are unconsciously fearful that if we begin to move away from our grief, we will lose what contact we have with the one we miss so much."* But maybe it is like letting go of one's children when they are ready to move off on their own. Perhaps the relinquishing of our most intense grief makes a space into which a new relationship with the loved one can move.

It is hard to face our fears, and night time is the worst. But, seemingly as a miracle, with the dawning of day, comes a better understanding and courage to face the day. However, if this is not the case with you, you may need to seek professional help if fears become overwhelming.

This is nothing to be ashamed of. It is OK.

This is an important quote for me and one I have shared with many, given to me by my niece (and adopted grandchild), Allyson:

> We cannot change the past,
> But we can ruin the present
> By worrying about the future.

*You gain strength, courage and confidence by every experience in which you really stop to look fear in the face . . . You must do the thing which you think you cannot do.*

—— Eleanor Roosevelt

## I Loved My Life

A friend once said to me, "I loved my life. I didn't want it to end." It truly touched me, because I felt the same. This is not true for everyone. This is OK too.

My husband's sister had a very domineering husband, but she still missed his presence when he was gone. After his death, she blossomed into a new person who discovered quilting and art and developed new friends. Another friend's husband was sick for ten years, slowly ebbing away at quality of life. She experienced her major grief while he was alive. Both of these women are amazing examples to others. REMEMBER THIS: We are all different. We all experience our own grief differently.

I once wrote to my husband's daughters that I realized with a sense of wonder and love and awe that I had lived a Christmas life with their father. To me this was the most beautiful analogy I could give them of their father, because Christmas has always been my favorite time of year.

I certainly did not mean this in the gift-giving manner. I meant it in the true spirit of Christmas, a life of special love and inspiring awe and gratefulness, and, most importantly, growth together in spirituality. Our priest at the time, Tim Murphy, once said in his final sermon, expressing his gratitude for the honor of burying our loved ones and, as he recounted the names of each of our loved ones buried: *Rudy Lane, soul mate of Beth Lane, for eternity.* What a compliment!

Regardless of your situation, I emphasis once again: Do NOT Compare; Do NOT Judge.

*Christmas: The bell still rings for all who truly believe.*

—— Polar Express

## ATTENTION SPAN

In the early period of our grief, we experience many things, including disorientation, loss of memory, lack of attention span, etc. This is NORMAL!

An avid reader, I went through three months (others have told me longer for them) after my husband died that I could not read. I found I just could not concentrate for any length of time. I kept thinking I "should" find solice in reading, even an escapism, but it would not come. This is perhaps the reason I found *Healing After Loss* so welcoming. It had extremely short and manageable day- by -day readings.

I wanted to read. I wanted the comfort of reading. (This was one of the pleasures my husband and I shared.) I also wanted the escapism it would bring. I could not force it. What I did not realize at the time was 'I' was not the same person and would never be again. I was beginning the path of a new identity. This not being able to concentrate was part of the whirling process of uncertainty of this new chapter.

I truly missed this simple pleasure also. Of all the things I could no longer experience, I felt I could and must retrieve this one. I thought perhaps if I read something I would not normally have read, it might change the tide. I chose *My Losing Season* by Pat Conroy. Although I had read all but one of his books, this one I would not have chosen. It was a true story of one year in his life at the Citadel and his basketball season. It was a book for Rudy, not for me. I pressed on and made it. The book was so good that I purchased several for Christmas presents, for our best friend, Allen Cooke, and two of the grandsons, A.W. Hamilton and Tyler Lowros. Some time later I encouraged two granddaughters to read it, Whitney Jeffers and Carrie Hamilton. Another grandson read it on his own, Jarad Hamilton. It became a book for all of us. We could see Rudy (PaPa) in the book!

The key is persevering. In Joan Didion's book, *The Year of Magical Thinking*, she thought she was going crazy. She brilliantly describes the illogical thinking that occurs during this time. She vividly describes illogical decisions made (not giving away all his clothes – he might need them; not giving away his shoes – he might need them) These were non-sensical thoughts, but ones I understood. My logical side said my husband would have chastised me, saying someone else could benefit from his clothes. My illogical side knew "I" needed them more at the time; this would be fully admitting he was never coming back. Life becomes persevering. We don't have a choice. Most of our 'crazy' thoughts we can't even admit to others at the time. 'We' even question ourselves at times. This is why I stress – you are NOT crazy. This too shall pass.

My friend, Charlotte, once said, "There is a three inch hole in my head where my brain used to be. The wind whips through and takes my memory with it." So aptly put.

*Grief is a pain so great that it is almost a physical presence inside you.*

—— Caroline Myss
*Invisible Acts of Power*

65

# HELPING OTHERS

After we have been 'pushed' into this new chapter of our life, we suddenly realize how little we have helped others in similar circumstances before now. Although we may chastise (to no avail, I might add) ourselves, over time we realize we could not have acted any differently; because we had not experienced it first hand.

The world takes on a different look in this new chapter. We suddenly realize how very unimportant most things are. We become an 'expert' on telling others to love more, hug more, and spend more quality time with your children and spouses. Will it work? Who knows. Only those who have experienced the 'worst' can truly see the small details of ordinary happiness.

How many times in the past have we said, Call me if there is anything I can do or help you with.

"Now" we know that call will just will *not* take place. We just do not have the energy to call; we want to be a hermit. "Now" we know WE are the ones who have to take the initiative. "Now" WE know WE are the ones who have to take charge and make things happen for the "W."

I was fortunate in having two close friends who pushed and pulled me out of the house and made me do things and go places. Although my daughters were extremely sensitive and included me in everything, as did their spouses, I did not want to take over their lives. I did not want to become a burden to them. In trying to take charge of my life again, I joined an EFM class at church. The goal was to make myself get out of the house at night. I achieved my goal and felt a victory after a year of Monday nights. I truly enjoyed the people; the Mentor was great, but my goal had been different from theirs.

Linda Feinberg wrote in *I'm Grieving As Fast As I Can*, "It has been said that the worst symptom of grief is that you can't see any light at the end of the tunnel." YOU can't see the light, but I am here to reassure you, there *is* light.

You have to find your own way in this New Chapter. I cannot stress strongly enough a *key* to your development is helping others, often anonymously. You will find you are changed in the process. Remember the quote from Dana Reeves, do it when you least feel like it. REMEMBER THIS: Be kind to yourself; be patient with yourself.

*Give because you want to touch someone.*

—— Alexandra Stoddard

# PERMISSION

Sometimes we are forced in life to drop our role we present to the world. Death is one of those times. In this vulnerable state, we are freer to receive the warmth and kindness of others. This is also a gift to our friends and family. Allowing them to help you, in any way, allows them to feel needed and express their love and concern.

We must give ourselves permission to be this vulnerable. It's OK to cry at inopportune times. It's OK to eat tomato soup for breakfast, as one friend said. It's OK to eat apples and cheese with wine for dinner (I survived for two and a half years on mostly this.). It's OK to say – NO – if you really don't feel like doing or going. It's OK to feel sorry for yourself (in the beginning). It's OK to not want to get out of bed (in the beginning – but do it anyway – it's the small steps that matter). It's OK to be depressed, but remember, you're the only one who can pull yourself out of depression.

Again, be kind to yourself. And again, don't compare how you are feeling or acting with anyone else. Remember, you don't know what's going on in someone else's head or behind their closed door.

The first year, almost without realizing it, we have a goal . . . *if* we can just get through that first year of 'firsts' and 'anniversaries' and special occasions. And then it's there. There is a sense of relief in knowing we have passed this first years of "firsts." Another friend shared with me after her first year anniversary: If I can get through this first year, I can do anything!

Please remember the "first year" is only a gauge. Many people experience much of what others go through after death during life, an ongoing battle during illness. This is also the reason I say – Do NOT Compare. Linda Feinberg said, "I don't even know what's normal anymore." This is also true for those who experience the slow death of quality of life during the living.

Know that you are your unique person and give yourself permission to react and act accordingly.

*We must learn to become comfortable in our new chapter, our new environment of one.*

—— epl

# THIS IS NOT ME

Many of the experiences or feelings I have talked about may not have happened to you. It's OK. There is no right or wrong way to feel; no timetable for grief.

A friend of mine in another state was besieged with health problems of her own, as well as family, after her husband died. It was not until a year later, on the first anniversary of his death, that she began to grieve. Unfortunately, her 'support group' had moved on with their lives. She was intelligent enough to realize what was happening, but she had no one to turn to. She had moved to another city and was beginning a new life without the one she loved most.

If you have had none of these feelings, you are fortunate. Do NOT think there is something wrong with you. Perhaps you have had all and more. In either case, REMEMBER THIS: you are not crazy!

I began this book to help others to know they are not alone in their feelings and actions and that they are not crazy as they experience the roller coaster emotions of grief. Many times over the time period I have written, I have felt this was all, and then along would come another passage. Sometimes another book recommended to me would prompt another passage. I don't feel these were accidents.

An out-of-print book was recommended to me by a young male

widower, who had happily remarried after several years. I have mentioned a couple of quotes from the book – Linda Feinberg's *I'm Grieving As Fast As I Can*. The title became his response when he was enundated with casseroles and advised to find a mother for his four children. A specialist in grief and loss therapy, Ms. Feinberg encourages my thought process:

*Consider yourself lucky if you don't have some or many of these symptoms. Don't worry about the ones you do have. You are not going crazy. You are in grief.*

I have written this book for myself, as much as for you. I am reaching out to those who need to be reassured, but I am also reassuring myself. I'm OK and each day I get better. I cannot speak to you as an expert or a professional on grief; I cannot even speak to you on women's grief. I can only speak to you of my grief and my path. Perhaps it will speak to your soul. If I can help one of you, then my sharing was as it should be. This is part of the new beginning, the New Chapter.


*Time removes all things but love and truth.*

—— Hall Whitworth

## SECOND CHANCE AT LIFE

In one of his last sermons at my home church, my priest, Tim Murphy, told a story of a woman in her nineties walking on the beach. She came across a man throwing star fish back into the ocean. She stopped walking and, in natural curiosity, asked the man if he was a collector. He replied, no, I'm giving them a second chance at life.

That is what we are being given. As we try to figure out who we are in this new and unwanted life, isn't this what God is giving us – a second chance? We've made it through the 'worst' (with His help). Now it's time for a new chapter, granted, unasked for and unwanted; but we're in it, no less. It is up to us to make the best of our second chance and, hopefully, to help someone else along the way.

You may be at a stage where this seems too daunting. That's OK. I think this is what friends and family do not fully realize, the utter scope of this immense loss is not just a person loved and now gone. To the spouse left behind, a part of their being has ended also. The loss is not only a physical loss, but also a loss of a relationship of togetherness, a loss of expectations of a future, and, as my brother Terry so aptly put it, a loss of the sheer energy of intertwined souls. Until one has experienced the stark uniqueness unto yourself, one cannot, and should not, fully understand the extent of the loss of your best friend, your lover, the father (step-father) to your children, your mentor, your confidant, your soul mate. The list seems bottomless and so void.

Rebuilding a new you, or even thinking about a second chance on life, does seem intimidating. We drift for a while, as the wind blows, taking one day at a time. At some point the wind becomes a cool breeze and the filtered light becomes gentle rays of sunshine. We suddenly realize --- we want to live!

What a tragedy it would be not to grab that thought and take those faltering steps into the sunshine. My home and heart are full of wonderful memories I do not want to lose or give up. The goal is to build on those, as a mentor would expect you to, as a loved one would want you to..

REMEMBER THIS: The rawness and intensity does lessen. It has to or we would not survive. It will be up to each of us to make the most of this Second Chance.

*My home . . . It had given me quiet, steady, demanding and undemanding seasons of pleasure. I took care of my home, then my home took care of me. Houses are patient with grief.*
—— Dominique Browning - *Around the House and In The Garden*

# OTHERS ARE GRIEVING TOO

Others really are grieving too. During the funeral time we all seem to reach out to each other. It is after we are alone that we feel we are the only ones in this isolated place. Later we realize others are and were grieving, just on a different level. We are all unique, and we all had a special and different relationship with the one who is now gone.

We must remember that friends grieve, just like family. And just like family, they don't know how to react to your grief, as they also try to deal with theirs. The difference is they, just like family, go back to their lives. They can compartmentalize or even 'disappear' their grief.

We also find that a good many of our friends disappear, not necessarily because they consciously want to, but because they simply do not know what to say or do. And YOU do not know how to help them help you, because *you* don't know how to help yourself either. The gray fog has rolled in, and it's heavy. It engulfs you, and you can't see through it.

Some close friends, some old and some new, are persistent. They become buoys, just like family. Much later you realize they were hurting too; but it's hard, if not impossible, to see through the fog of grief to help anyone else. Your fog has become more dense.

If there are children, brothers or sisters, mothers or fathers, you must share this time with them, for their grief is great too. The caretaker in you usually kicks in during this time of suspension. The funeral sometimes becomes almost like a party. It is and should be a celebration of your loved one's life, as memories and laughter are shared. This is good, because the pain is held at bay for time periods. It is a cleansing for all.

Each person's grief is unique unto that individual, not only because they are unique, but also because their relationship with the individual was also. Again, the major difference in their space of grief and yours is they will go home to resume their life with spouses, children, friends, jobs. They still have their grief, but they have to, again, compartmentalize it according to responsibilities. Their lives immediately become busy and full, with 'normal.'

You are the one who is now 'half' of a whole, living in an empty house of memories. Depression is there for all of us. It is the dealing with it day by day that helps us to get through the period of fog. We know it will lift; we just don't know when. There is no timetable and no way to speed the natural order. The fog comes and goes and comes again.

Many times these other grieving persons, family and friends alike, reach a point where they feel they have adequately dealt with their grief and wonder why you have not. Sometimes they even verbalize this to you. I know it is hard, but try not to take offense.

REMEMBER THIS: They have not yet been in the place where you stand. They are well meaning; they just do not know. Remember my words: Do NOT judge; Do NOT compare.

*If you could only sense how important you are to the lives of those you meet; how important you can be to the people you may never even dream of. There is something of yourself that you leave at every meeting with another person.*

—— Fred Rogers
*The World According to Mister Rogers*

## WHERE DO WE FIND GOD (AGAIN)?

I said this was not a religious book; however, I would be terribly remiss without this section because I do believe this book was God inspired and directed.

I find God in the early morning hours.

Years ago our priest (and best friend), Allen Cooke, suggested we 'take on' something, rather than giving up something for Lent. I began to get up an hour earlier (at that time in my life my daughters were still in school and there seemed to be no other time in my busy life) to read the Bible. Another Lent I 'tried' to write a note to someone everyday (this one took several Lents to fulfill).

You guessed it! This became a precious habit. It became my time with God. I would sit in the living room early in the morning, with coffee, read, and pray. After my husband died, I established a new routine. I had coffee in bed with God each morning. I still do this. My time with God has lengthened each morning, as we share readings from different books.

God has sustained me. He has often carried me. I cannot imagine going through 'the worst' without Him by my side. Perhaps you are not there yet. Perhaps you have not 'talked' with God in a long time (or ever). Perhaps you are angry with God. All of this is OK. All it takes to turn the corner is desire. Just listen. God is there.

Marlo Thomas wrote in her second book, *The Right Words at the Right Time*, of a young woman whose husband had died of cancer, leaving her alone with an eleven year old son. With a 'shakey' relationship with God, she picked out a synagogue in the Yellow Pages and went there and screamed and yelled at God for an hour, venting her anger. Afterwards she went to the Rabbi and told him what she had done and how guilty she felt. He smiled gently and said, "At least it's a relationship." Another story in her book was of a young Catholic woman whose faith and training had begun to unravel when she had gone off to college. Sitting alone in church, questioning if there is a God, a nun sat down beside her and listened to her turmoil. After her speel, the nun asked softly, " Do you believe in people, in their being born with good intentions?" The young woman replied, "I think so." The nun gave her these words, "Then you believe in God. That's good enough for now."

The point is – your anger is OK. "At least it's a relationship. That's good enough for now."

Jerry Sittser lost his wife, his daughter, and his mother in a tragic car accident. He was left to raise three young children, as well as rebuild his own life. He wrote in his book, *A Grace Disguised*, " My faith did not begin with the accident. Still, since then I have grown spiritually in new ways."

My husband and I grew together spiritually. I have had to learn to grow singularly. I have made new friends doing so, as well as deeper friendships with others. Try it. You won't be alone.

*Learn to live one day at a time. By an act of your will, choose to start enjoying your life right now. Enjoy everything in your life.*

—— Joel Osteen

# WHAT CAN "I" DO?

For those of you who would ask, "So what can I do?" I would say –
just be there. You, too, should not judge or compare.

I saved this reading from a *Day by Day*:

*Our culture wants to push people through despair, depression, grief.*
*"Get over it," we say (or think) when someone else's suffering makes us*
*uncomfortable. But sometimes we are called to simply **be** . . . to be with*
*someone in the midst of anguish, without trying to solve the situation.*

*Sometimes the hardest thing to do is simply to stand still, not to turn*
*away, not to run away from another's passion or pain. Be there. Just be*
*there.*

Just be a friend. Realize the importance of friendship. Help someone
else. I saved this quote a good friend sent:

*Each friend represents a world in us, a world possibly not born until*
*they arrive, and it is only by this meeting that a new world is born.*

—— Anais Nir

83

*God speaks to us in many ways . . . Listen to the Whispers*

—— epl

# JOY

Will I ever know joy again?

Listen to me and know what I say is true. Yes, joy does return. Just as I have said, one day you wake up and "know" you want to live; one day you will realize you have suddenly experienced 'joy' in a happening or person. It is a turning point.

Just as we are creating a new life, in this new chapter, in this second chance of life, our joy will no doubt be different too. We must find this new joy ourselves – outside the realm of caregiving. As we learn to give care to ourselves, we have to listen carefully for a new awakening of joy – joy in the ordinary, i.e., growing a garden, cooking gourmet meals, painting, writing, returning to school, volunteering, helping someone else, helping ourselves . . . stepping out-of-our box.

Pamela Peeks uses 'joy' as a verb, asking her patients to pay attention to daily joys by saying, *"So – Have you joyed yourself today?"*

Begin to develop new rituals – just for you!

-Have a Tea Time – just for you

-Start a 'walking' group

-Plan mini trips with different people

-Start a book club

-Try a new recipe once a week (month)

-Go out to lunch/dinner with someone new

-Do something anonymously for someone else

-Be creative – step out-of-your box

"Joy" yourself today!

*Giving anonymously is divine.*

—— Alexandra Stoddard

## A New Beginning

Linda Feinberg wrote, "I don't even know what's normal anymore." We all know the truth of that statement. We have to develop a new 'normal.' I am beginning my Third Life. I owe it to myself to make it the best life I can. I owe it to the memory of my husband to enhance the personal growth that we shared and to go beyond. This is a big year for me, and this book is my personal gift to myself. It has taken me awhile to get to this place, but that's OK too.

REMEMBER this quote that has been so hard for me:

> We must be willing to get rid of the life we've planned,
> So as to have the life that is waiting for us.
>
> —— Joseph Campbell

At a recent wedding of a nephew, the groom's father and my brother, Mike (a Baptist minister), prayed that they have "an interesting journey" together. I like that. Let's make this life, this second chance, an interesting journey too.

Cassandra King wrote in *Queen of Broken Hearts*, *"What have we learned about loss during our time together? Hopefully we've found that loss is always a journey of self-discovery. And now we know that the journey has not ended; It has just begun."*

87

*Listen to the Whispers . . .*

—— epl

# AND SO . . .

I would like to express my sincere gratitude to all whose words I have borrowed to enhance my work, for in those words, I have found solace. I hope you do also. May we all help someone else.

In January of 2006, a friend gave me some statistics she had read. In a year, 700,000 become widows. Of those, 30,000 remarry.

REMEMBER THIS: That is only 2%. This is a strong argument for rebuilding ourselves as individuals.

For some years now, our church has compiled a pamphlet of meditations for Lent, written by lay volunteers and based on four Biblical verses for that day. During the last years of his life, my husband chose to participate with a Good Friday writing. He ended with this:

*Today is the day that Jesus died for us; and, because of this, our own death is not an ending but a new beginning, not a day of sorrow but one of celebration, and not a day of remorse but one of thanksgiving. Thanks be to God!*

His favorite Bible verse: *I can do all things through Christ who strengthens me.* Phil. 4:13

. . . . . . . . . . . . . . . . . . . . . . . . . . .

The quotes I give in this book and at the end that I have shared with you have touched a part of me at some point in my life. They were given to me at times when I needed them.

REMEMBER THIS: Just because something speaks to me, it may not be speaking to you. That's OK. When I give a special book to a friend, I also say, if it doesn't speak to you now, lay it aside and pick it up at a later date. Time travels differently for all.

*Listen to the Whispers . . .*

—— epl

*You make your own happiness.*

—— Rudy Lane

# Notes

It is with gratitude that I note the following writings that have traveled with me on my journey.

Dominique Browning
*Around the House and In The Garden*

Always . . . my Day by Day readings

Lisa Gardner
*Gone* (novel)

Margaret Whitmore Hickman
*Healing After Loss* (given to me by Adrienne Ford)
This book has been read three times in full and many times in highlight; it has been given to many others in need.

Roger Housden
*Seven Sins For a Life Worth Living*

Cassandra King
*Queen of Broken Hearts* (novel)

Charlotte King
*A Letter to Friends*

Caroline Myss
*Invisible Acts of Power*

Oprah
*"O" Magazine*

Joel Osteen
*Your Best Life Now* — Book and Journal
(given to me by Beth Jeffers)

Don Piper
*90 Minutes in Heaven*
(given by Beth Jeffers)

Nora Roberts
*Black Rose* (novel)
*Divided in Death* (novel)

Florence Scovel Shinn
*The Wisdom of Florence Scovel Shinn*
(recommended by Wendy Van Pelt Gautney)

Jerry Sittser
*A Grace Disguised*
(recommended by Jan Hardeman)

Marlo Thomas
*The Right Words at the Right Time*
(discovered on a visit to granddaughter, Whitney Jeffers, in
Oxford, Mississippi)

C.S. Lewis
*A Grief Observed*
(recommended by Barbara Broach)

Joan Didion
*The Year of Magical Thinking*
(recommended by Barbara Broach)

Alexandra Stoddard
*ALL 23 books*
(especially — *Choosing Happiness*)
given by Paige and Robyn

Suffice it to say, these need listing; however, truth be known, and after the first three months, many, many books and authors could be listed. For those who truly enjoy reading, you will understand — books are friends, friends who bring healing.

*Angels Unaware . . . Thank God for things that happen without reason.*

*— epl*

*Footsteps in the Sand by Terry M. Purdy*

*Listen to the Whispers . . .*

97

All Doodles by
Kyle Age 9

# The Wolf Who Cried Boy

By:
Mary Jean Hughes, Ed.D.

Illustrator:
Kyle Gillen-Hughes

# Intention

This book is based on a true story
(please read disclaimer).
The intent of this book is to inform and educate
families about a condition called dyslexia that
affects 10 million children in the United States.
(Shaywitz). This author believes this book contains
information about what every parent
should know about advocacy.

©Text copyright: 2008 by Mary Jean Hughes
©Illustrations copyright: 2008 Kyle Gillen-Hughes
©Foreword copyright: 2008 Andrew S. McAleer
Editor: Michael J. Rielly
Graphic Design: Cherry Bishop
Special Assistance: The Kelly Family, Heidi Vincent

Mary Jean Hughes is a new literary agent.

---

### Disclaimer

*The Wolf Who Cried Boy* is a true account. However, some names and details may have been changed in order to protect all those involved. The main purpose of writing this book is to educate and support struggling children and parents.

---

ISBN: 978-0-615-14172-5
Published by Sheridan Books, Inc., Ann Arbor, Michigan.
Printed in the United States of America.

# Dedication

This book is dedicated to
Bridie & Gordon Hughes, and
Hunna & Moe Gillen,
with love and admiration.

It is through these wonderful parents
and people that I learned how to advocate,
and to become hungry for education and justice.

Also, this author would like to thank the
following people for their expertise and support:
Andrew S. McAleer,
for putting up with all of my E-mails, and for his
continuous words of encouragement, and
Michael Rielly,
for helping me become a more critical writer and
offering me support and guidance along the way.
I would also like to thank
Cherry Bishop, The Kelly Family, Heidi Vincent,
Steve Muench, Steve Wilkins and Dr. Karen Jacobs.

# Table of Contents

**Foreword** ..................................................................... xi

**Introduction** ............................................................ xvii

**Chapter 1** ..................................................................... 1
Pre-School Years

**Chapter 2** .....................................................................7
Kindergarten Years

**Chapter 3** ................................................................. 17
First Grade

**Chapter 4** .................................................................57
Second Grade

**Chapter 5** .................................................................69
The Process

**Family Photo Album**

**Summary** ...................................................................91

**Epilogue** ................................................................. 105

**Author's Notes**....................................................... 111

**Notes & Reminders** ..............................................115

# Foreword

## The Wolf Who Cried Boy

In a recent study by the Harvard Graduate School of Education under the guidance of Professor Tami Katzir, it was observed that "close to 40 percent of U.S. fourth-grade children score below grade level in reading assessments, according to the National Center for Education Statistics. And it is estimated that 10 percent to 15 percent of children have been diagnosed with dyslexia, a learning disability signaled by serious difficulty in reading, writing, and spelling."

Now that dyslexia has, in some measure, been identified quantitatively in the United States with respect to children, the question presented ought to be how educators address this condition during a child's early development.

Although not a plenary study on the American educational system in this particular area, *The Wolf Who Cried Boy* does chronicle one mother's (Mary Jean Hughes, who ironically holds a Doctorate in Education) seemingly endless struggle to obtain the necessary educational services required for her son Kyle.

Dr. Hughes tells us that Kyle's school, despite the voluminous amount of well-documented psychological evidence of his dyslexic condition, again and again

# Foreword

(continued)

delayed and denied him essential services. Why might this be so?

When we consider objectively these staggering figures propounded by Harvard, it would be remiss to ignore as one possible suspect: the lack of Special Education funding. Because of their already inadequate budget allotments, the thought of administering special programs for the legions of dyslexic children is an expense many public and private schools cannot entertain seriously.

As a consequence, unless the proper programs are set into place, then the solutions are to: "pass these children along in school" and wish them luck, or to change the way society views dyslexia in order to obtain adequate funding. Thankfully, Dr. Hughes is not alone in her quest to bring this important subject matter to the fore.

At the Center for the Study of Dyslexia and Talent, a program of the Krasnow Institute for Advanced Study at George Mason University, the Institute focuses on the possible advantages of dyslexia rather than the public stigmas often associated with dyslexia. Their philosophy is expressed thusly:

"The Center is primarily interested in investigating the apparent associations between dyslexia and the visual and other non-verbal talents that many dyslexics seem to exhibit. Some argue that these talents are accidental and have no direct connection to dyslexia (or other similar learning differences).

"However, other researchers argue that the very early changes in brain development and structure experienced by dyslexics can also produce a varied range of attributes, some of which can be quite positive and advantageous.

"Our studies are designed to clarify these preliminary case-study observations. Our long-term expectation is that education and employment expectations and practices will be significantly affected by the results of these studies."

*The Wolf Who Cried Boy* discusses a daring topic. This is a true story told by a loving mother who experienced "delay and denial" from the very system that was supposed to offer assistance and guidance.

# Foreword

(continued)

Fortunately, however, the roadblocks Dr. Hughes encountered while advocating for her son now serve as an essential roadmap for anyone who seeks the proper, Special Educational services necessary for his or her child. With this book at your side, no parent or child faced with similar issues should feel alone. The reader will experience firsthand what it is like to deal with school officials, Special Education instructors, and the importance of hiring a qualified educational advocate and attorney.

Finally, *The Wolf Who Cried Boy* exhibits Kyle's talent as an artist through some of his wonderful drawings. Drawings, I hope, that will give the powers-that-be cause for deep reflection.

**Andrew S. McAleer, J.D.**
McGuinn Hall, Boston College, 2008

Andrew McAleer is the best-selling author of four books, an intern at the May Institute in Boston, and a Master's in Counseling Psychology candidate at the Massachusetts School of Professional Psychology.

# Introduction

Ironically when I typed "introduction" the first time, I mistakenly typed "introducation."

This will make sense as you read the book. Hopefully, this book will be a cathartic experience as it assists parents tasked with identifying the Special Education needs of their child or children.

Moreover, I am hopeful this book can teach parents of twice-gifted children how to **advocate** for their offspring within the public education system. Let me first start out by explaining that I am a strong proponent of public schools for regular education services, but NOT for Special Education services.

My reasoning is based on my personal experience that is carefully documented in this book.

My name is Mary Jean, and I hold a Doctorate in Education (leadership in schooling), a Master's Degree in Community Psychology, and a Bachelor's Degree in Occupational Therapy, all from prestigious universities.

As you read this book, you will realize why I reference my spelling and grammar so often.

# Introduction

(continued)

However, I am hopeful it will not be reflected on the pages in this book due to good editing and my perserverence (oops, there I go again with a misspelled word).

There are so many thoughts racing through my head about the organization and direction of this introduction that I am just going with the flow. But the good news is, I do have an outline for the rest of the book.

If you are a person who knows about dyslexia, you may be thinking "I get the feeling that this author has dyslexic symptoms or is dyslexic." Although never formally diagnosed, I am convinced that I have dyslexia.

My 10-year-old son Kyle has dyslexia and surprise, surprise—my father had dyslexia. A couple of my sisters, and some of my nieces and nephews, have dyslexia. Are we noticing a pattern here? Of course there is a pattern.

We now know that dyslexia affects one out of every five children—10 million children in America alone (Shaywitz). Considering I am one of nine children, the fact that some of my sisters have dyslexia is consistent with this research. It is reassuring that we are not flukes of nature.

Dyslexia is not only common; it is persistent (Shaywitz). This might explain why I can write a comprehensive occupational therapy evaluation, and keep detailed treatment records, but I am often unable to come up with the correct word when I need it.

This phenomenon also helps this author understand that although I was always an A student who was accepted to excellent universities, I consistently had difficulty with multiple-choice tests—unless they had no time limit.

People who have dyslexia are very good at describing what they want to say. I have to give credit where credit is due. If it were not for the book that Sally Shaywitz, M.D., wrote, and the research she completed, I would still be struggling as to why my son Kyle and I are so different. Or at least, why we often feel so different because of how our dyslexia allows us to learn and process information.

The first clue to dyslexia may be a delay in speaking (Shaywitz). My son and I both had speech therapy for approximately two years when we were four years old. While a delay in speaking may be familial, so is dyslexia (Shaywitz). It is now possible to test young children (optimally, at around four or five years of age) for early indicators of dyslexia. Children with family histories of

# Introduction

reading disability should be standing right in the front of the line for such testing (Shaywitz).

As you read this book, you will learn about a 43-year-old mother, and a gifted young boy. You will bear witness to his early and present struggles with dyslexia, as well as his triumphs and the wonderful school that he currently attends.

To give you just a hint about what prompted me to write this book, I went from painstakingly watching my seven-year-old son cry before school and after school—and watching him shiver in fear during classroom curriculum activities—to feeling good about himself and yes, even looking forward to school days. I always thought kids should be "skipping to school" in first grade, never to feel the weight of the world on their shoulders (boy was I wrong).

For those readers out there, similar to myself, who have difficulty keeping track of multiple dates, times and details, I have included a timeline related to Kyle's development. The timeline begins in pre-school, runs through third grade, and chronicles our journey for justice.

In addition, when I refer to "we" in the story, this author is referring to Kyle's loving parents, both of whom agreed on decisions related to Kyle's interventions, schooling, and legal rights.

# Approximate Time Line

- **Fall 1989**

  Kyle is three years and four months old. He attends a pre-school program.

- **Fall 1990**

  Kyle is four years and four months old. He continues to attend the pre-school program. Private speech and language interventions begin.

- **Fall 1991**

  Kyle is five years and two months old. He begins full-day private kindergarten. Also, a public school speech and language therapist begins to treat Kyle.

- **Fall 1992**

  Kyle is six years and two months old. He begins his second-year in full-day private kindergarten. Private occupational therapy interventions begin.

  Neuropsychologist #1 observes Kyle on lead teacher's recommendation. Also, a private Ph.D. completes a reading assessment, and private 1:1 (one-to-one) reading tutorial services begin.

- **August 1993**

  We request a Reading Assessment from the public school. Private occupational therapy interventions continue.

# Approximate Time Line

(continued)

- **Fall 1993**
  Kyle is seven years and two months old. He begins private first grade with a class size of 16 children and two teachers. The public school reading assessment is completed and a meeting occurs to discuss the results.

- **Fall 1993**
  Kyle is seven years and three months old.
  He transitions from private first grade to public first grade.

- **Fall 1993**
  We request full CORE Evaluation from public school.

- **Winter 1994**
  First Individual Educational Plan (IEP) Eligibility Meeting occurs. Meeting with the head of Special Education occurs. Kyle participates in evaluation(s) with neuropsychologist #2 at our expense.

- **Spring 1994**
  Second and Third IEP Eligibility Meetings occur.

- **Summer 1994**
  Mediation occurs.

- **Fall 1994**
  Kyle is eight years and two months old. He begins second grade at a private school. He participates in evaluation with neuropsychologist #3 at our expense.

- **Summer 1995**
  Fourth IEP Eligibility Meeting occurs.

- **Fall 1995**
  Kyle is nine years and two months old. He begins third grade at a private school.

- **Spring 1996**
  Resolution Conference occurs. People present at the conference are: mediator, head of Special Education, the public school attorney, parents, and parents' attorney.

Artist: Kyle, Age 5

# Chapter 1

"You should prefer a good scientist without literary
abilities than a literate without scientific skills."

**Leonardo da Vinci**

## Pre-School Years

I am thinking, do I want to start from today, when Kyle is 10 years old—and work my way back to when he was three years old? After all, the warning signs started right about at age three.

Or do I want to begin our story when Kyle was three years old—and work forward to today?

This uncertainty is another trait people with dyslexia have—always wondering which direction they should go. I also notice that sometimes my sisters will reverse parts of their speech, as well as my son and myself—for example, the title of this book.

Another trait I have noticed is that people with dyslexia are great at making up words. This past summer I said "Please hand me that can, I want to put it on the lazy souza." The person I asked said, "What did you say?"

So I repeated "Please hand me that can, I want to put it on the lazy souza." The person I was conversing with said, "It is a lazy Susan, not a lazy souza." I said, "Oh. I've been calling it a lazy souza for as long as I can remember."

With all of that said, I have made an executive decision to begin Kyle's story when he was three years old, and work forward to today.

I am doing this because more positive actions happen at the end of our journey than at the beginning, and I want to end with the positive. Unfortunately, a lot of negative experiences occurred during this arduous process.

If people can learn from the mistakes that I illustrate, and I can help one struggling student and family, then writing this book will be worthwhile.

When Kyle was approximately three-and-a-half years old, he started going to a pre-school program in our town. As a new mother with two sons, I thought my boys were just about perfect. The first clue that something might be amiss came when Kyle's pre-school teacher told me that he did not always take the most direct path with his actions.

I thought, "O.K., I'm an occupational therapist (OT), I can figure this out." So I started to watch him more closely. When I witnessed Kyle completing a gross motor task, I thought, "His teacher is correct. His motor planning is different than his classmates', and different from his little brother's."

I also started to suspect that his auditory processing was different. For example, I had to repeat directions frequently to Kyle.

Our home is filled with books, and although I had to work very hard in school, I did not anticipate there would be a problem with Kyle's learning.

Also, my late mother loved reading to Kyle and Liam, who is Kyle's younger brother. She would stay with us during the week when I was in the doctoral program.

Kyle's pre-school program included different activities such as gym and swim opportunities. When we were in swim class one morning at the end of the year the teacher asked him, "What is your name?"

And Kyle said "Kyle," but it sounded like "Tyler" due to an articulation delay.

At this point I thought "He is almost four years old. He should be seen by a speech and language pathologist because he is not articulating as well as he should be."

Please keep in mind that although I was already an OT at the time, I was also a fairly new mother. So this realization was difficult to accept.

Subsequently, I had my son evaluated at the Valley Hospital Speech and Language Department. Kyle was now four years and four months old.

His auditory comprehension was measured at the age-equivalent of three years and 10 months, and his expressive communication was measured at the age-equivalent of three years and nine months.

Therefore, some delays in Kyle's development were clearly identified, and it was time for official early intervention to begin. We began working on improving Kyle's speech production skills with his family, his peers, and with other adults in the home, school and clinic environments.

The speech and language pathologist from Valley Hospital recommended that Kyle work 60 minutes weekly for six months, and Kyle began to make good progress with his speech.

Studies show that dyslexia does not have to prevent a person from succeeding. There are numerous successful artists, scientists and business executives who have dyslexia.

Some experts say that because the brains of people who have dyslexia are wired a little differently, they may often problem solve in much more innovative ways.

Artist: Kyle, Age 6

# Chapter 2

"I hated school...One of the reasons was a learning disability, dyslexia, which no one understood at the time. I still can't spell..."

**Loretta Young**

## Kindergarten Years

The following fall, Kyle began a full-day private kindergarten at a prestigious New England university. I also had him evaluated by our hometown school speech and language pathologist. She noted some delays in his development, and recommended treating Kyle two times a week for 30 minutes.

So at this point, Kyle was receiving speech therapy three times a week for a total of two hours—one hour with a private speech and language pathologist, and two half-hour sessions with the public school speech and language pathologist.

Furthermore, his private speech and language pathologist reevaluated Kyle, and determined an additional six months of speech and language sessions, with 60-minute weekly sessions, would benefit him.

Subsequently, I informed Kyle's new kindergarten teacher about the speech and language interventions Kyle was now receiving. In the middle of Kyle's first year in full-day kindergarten, his teacher told me that Kyle was struggling with organization of information. At the end of the school year, it was recommended that he repeat kindergarten.

During his second year in full-day kindergarten, when Kyle was six years old, I continued to notice some gross motor and fine motor delays. So I brought him to participate in an occupational therapy evaluation. These tests were scheduled for two three-hour sessions, and the occupational therapist (OT) asked me to bring Kyle a snack.

Although I was a practicing OT myself, it was and still is difficult to provide OT interventions with Kyle. For that matter, I think it would be difficult for any parent and child.

As you can imagine, I love Kyle too much to watch him struggle, and it is difficult to be impartial.

Following the first part of the occupational therapy evaluation, the OT spoke with me in private when Kyle was taking a break and enjoying his snack. She stated, "I'm glad you brought him in. He is experiencing some vestibular problems."

At this point my mind went blank. My brain felt like it was not operating. Although I was a practicing OT at the time, I couldn't remember what "vestibular involvement" was.

Another trait people with dyslexia have in common is that when we want to think of something (or recall) there is sometimes a blank.

Or, as Kyle describes it, "a white out."

The OT finished the evaluation with Kyle, and then it comes to me. "Oh yes! The vestibular system has to do with movement and the balance sense which responds to stimuli processed at receptor sites located in the inner ear."

At the end of the OT's evaluation, she determined that Kyle had difficulty with the organization and sequencing of higher-level skills and complex motor tasks—particularly with sequencing tasks or using multiple stimuli during challenges.

Kyle struggled with multi-step tasks that required working memory. The OT noted that this could have significant impact on his ability to organize sequences and complete academic assignments that require integrating several processes.

The OT recommended that Kyle receive occupational therapy treatment for a minimum of one one-hour session per week for remediation of the delays noted.

At this point, Kyle was participating in skilled speech and language therapy, as well as occupational therapy.

Early intervention was in full swing.

At the beginning of his second year in full-day kindergarten, Kyle began to feel the academic pressure.

He became very good at memorizing books, but often wondered what would happen if someone doesn't learn to read. He told me, "The words mix up my brain."

I tried to take the pressure off by telling him, "Kyle, do not be worried, because some kids don't read until third of fourth grade." I said to him, "You are smart and kind. Do not worry too much about reading."

In the middle of his second year in full-day kindergarten, the concerns about Kyle's academic progress and reading readiness continued.

Because we had him in a private kindergarten at a large university—which has a specialty major in early childhood education, reading and literacy—we asked for a Ph.D. who worked in this program to assess Kyle.

During this evaluation, the Ph.D. noted that Kyle had trouble blending letters to form rhymes. This ability to rhyme is necessary for children to move beyond emergent reading and begin decoding print. For most kindergarteners (who are about age five), it's not a concern if they can't rhyme. At the same time, many children this age can do rhyming.

At age six-and-a-half, when most children are halfway through the first grade, this inability to rhyme was definitely something that warranted further investigation.

So we continued with the early intervention. In fact, Kyle started to see a wonderful 1:1 (one-to-one) reading tutor following his assessment by the Ph.D. His 1:1 reading tutor was a professional and competent reading teacher who objectively was able to analyze the data and provide great assistance to Kyle.

In the meantime, it was reassuring for us to read about all the wonderful things Kyle was accomplishing in his kindergarten experience. Private schools love to highlight the positives!

However, due to Kyle's continued delays and difficulties, and because this was his second year in a full-day kindergarten, it was recommended by his lead teacher, and the director, that a neuropsychologist observe Kyle during his kindergarten day and spend some time with him. Due to his difficulties, I thought this was a good idea, too.

It should be noted that this was the first of three neuropsychologists to observe our son. This initial encounter with a neuropsychologist was very informal; therefore, later on in Kyle's development, we decided to hire two additional neuropsychologists, where our experience would be much more formal.

Although we never received a written report from the first neuropsychologist, we did sit down with her, and she told us that Kyle was indeed struggling with the organization of information. For example, it takes him extra time to process what he is hearing, and to develop his ideas into a verbal response.

However, given sufficient time, the questions Kyle asks are pertinent to the topic at hand. Often it takes a second reading or more verbalization for Kyle to be able to comprehend what is said or read to him. But he is able to comprehend what he sees and hears when given the necessary supports.

Kyle is also able to follow directions as long as they are clear, or they have been repeated for clarification. She also shared with us that Kyle is extremely intelligent, and that was reassuring to hear as a parent!

It is now near the end of Kyle's second year in full-day kindergarten. We are very concerned about the large class sizes in the public schools; therefore, we enroll him in a private first grade class of 16 children with two teachers at the private university.

As well, due to Kyle's continued OT needs, we decide to have him participate in continued OT services—which included approximately 47 days of an OT dynamic listening program.

At the end of these sessions, Kyle exhibited improved vestibular processing, motor speed and bilateral coordination.

This progress was demonstrated by improved response to movement, standing and walking balance, motor response time, and coordination of the two sides of his body during jumping, hopping, and pumping a swing.

Recommendations included that he should still receive a minimum of one 60-minute session or two 30-minute sessions of occupational therapy per week to support his vestibular, visual/spatial, and developmental hand skills.

In addition, the OT thought Kyle was experiencing some eye teaming problems, and recommended that we see a developmental optometrist.

At this point, Kyle has finished his second year in full day kindergarten, and is about to start in his private first grade class.

Because we were still concerned, and the many private interventions were so costly, we decided to have Kyle participate in a reading assessment with the public schools reading specialist. In August, prior to first grade, I spoke to Mr. Davis, who was the principal of the public elementary school. He informed me that I had to request this reading assessment in writing, which I did.

Artist: Kyle, Age 7

Chapter 3

"He told me that his teachers reported that...
he was mentally slow, unsociable, and
adrift forever in his foolish dreams."

**Hans Albert Einstein**, on his father, Albert Einstein

# First Grade

We are still very concerned about Kyle and his learning.

At this point, the public school reading specialist, Ms. Jenkins, was completing the reading assessment with Kyle, and promised the results soon.

In the meantime, I also scheduled an evaluation with a behavioral optometrist in November due to the OT's concerns and recommendation.

When you have a child with dyslexia, there is no time to rest in the early years of his or her academic involvement. This is because more and more research indicates that early intervention is the most optimal. It is much better for a child to develop learning strategies and reading skills the correct way—versus having to undo all kinds of inappropriate learning, not to mention the damage this can do to a child's self esteem!

The results of the reading evaluation from the public school reading specialist, Ms. Jenkins, were very concerning. His scores were well below his age and grade placement in several areas. It was my first impression that Ms. Jenkins was a competent reading specialist, and that she wanted to show off her talents as the new reading specialist in town.

Unfortunately, as the story progresses, although Ms. Jenkins was a competent reading specialist, she did not advocate for Kyle to receive the individualized educational services that he desperately required.

My interpretation, as well as that of others, was that Kyle has dyslexia. However, the word "dyslexic" was never used by any of the public school staff.

Why?

Maybe because dyslexia is an accepted disability, which requires individualized educational services?

I used to wonder, "Ms. Jenkins understands the complexities of dyslexia, so why isn't she Kyle's 'number one' advocate, and working with his parents?"

In order to find out, after the results of the evaluation were completed, we scheduled a meeting with the principal of the public elementary school, Mr. Davis. We also asked that the public school reading specialist, Ms. Jenkins; the private first grade teacher, Ms. Sarah; and the private school director, Ms. O'Leary, all attend the meeting.

During the meeting, Ms. Jenkins, the person who administered the reading evaluations, was recommending that Kyle receive reading services with her, three times a week.

We asked, "Can Kyle receive these services at the start of the day?" The response was "No!"

It was physically impossible for anyone, much less a working parent, to take Kyle from his private school, up to the public elementary school for the reading intervention, and then back again.

Also, the private school's personnel told us that they did not have a structured phonics program to meet Kyle's needs. Surprisingly, the public school program contained more of the services and structure that Kyle would need.

Shortly after our meeting, we decided to pull Kyle from his private first grade (losing approximately $5,000) and enroll him in the public elementary school, where he would receive reading instruction three times a week with the reading specialist.

Also at our meeting, we shared with the group that Kyle had recently participated in an occupational therapy evaluation—and that in-school skilled OT services were recommended.

The transition from private school to public school was a surprise to all, we believe. Maybe this is cynical thinking; however, we do not believe Ms. Jenkins thought we would pull Kyle from private school and put him in a public one.

But as a parent with a child who has Special Education needs, you should be constantly providing early intervention, looking through the data, and considering the most appropriate program(s) available to your child.

This continual search for the correct services is exhausting, but it's crucial to a child's development! One big positive during this difficult time was the emergence of Kyle's enjoyment of art. He loved to sketch, and was quite gifted at it.

Although I am his mother and biased, of course, I also realized his drawings didn't look like those of other first-graders. Kyle's were more advanced.

One day I asked Kyle, "Do you want to take art classes?" He said he did, so I started to look for art teachers who could give him lessons. It took some time, but Kyle started art lessons the following spring with a wonderful artist.

It took time to find an art teacher for Kyle because I wanted to make sure he or she would be able to address his special needs, especially giving him encouragement. Kyle's art teacher ended up being more than capable. She was wonderful!

Regarding Kyle's public school transition, prior to Kyle starting at his new elementary school, I conveyed to the Principal, Mr. Davis, all of Kyle's Special Education needs. I also provided for Mr. Davis and Ms. Connors, Kyle's new first grade teacher, all of Kyle's occupational therapy, speech therapy and school reports from the private university program.

I wanted to make sure they were aware of all Kyle's learning differences so they could give Kyle the assistance he needed.

So, Kyle joined his new public first grade class at the end of September 1993. After Kyle's first day, he came to me in tears and said:

"I had the worst day of my whole life and I hate school."

I still can recall that sick feeling I had in my stomach when I heard this, all the while trying to stay positive with my gifted little boy, and keep that spark for learning burning.

Also after Kyle's first day, Ms. Connors told us that it was a hard day for Kyle, and she asked whether we planned on requesting a full CORE evaluation. A CORE evaluation is a comprehensive set of evaluations administered by various professionals.

Later that same week we requested, and attended, a meeting with Ms. Connors. She again asked us whether we would be requesting a CORE evaluation. We said "yes," but we wanted to wait a few weeks until Kyle could adjust to his new school.

A few weeks later we requested, in writing, a full CORE evaluation from the public school. The CORE evaluation was conducted during the next several months, with the last assessment taking place on April 24, 1994.

The CORE evaluation consisted of an initial evaluation, an academic evaluation, a psychological evaluation, and initial occupational therapy evaluations—as well as a follow-up evaluation due to the need to further investigate Kyle's sensory integration abilities as reported by the evaluator.

This development of further OT testing was interesting due to the fact that during our initial meeting, where we discussed the results of the reading evaluation, I shared with the group that Kyle's private occupational therapist recommended skilled occupational therapy (OT) services in-school.

In response, the Principal, Mr. Davis, said that because the private OT testing was so recent, I should submit it to the head of Special Education—and those services may be provided. I did submit the private OT evaluation after the meeting. However, the recommendation to implement skilled OT services in-school for Kyle was denied partially based on the fact that Mr. Grady, Head of Special Education for the public school, reserved the right to have a public school OT complete an evaluation. As a result, he determined the private OT evaluation would not be accepted in lieu of a public school OT evaluation.

On another front, after meeting with the behavioral optometrist, she recommended a program of optometric vision therapy to assist Kyle with improving his visual efficiency and visual information processing abilities.

She also completed a dyslexic screening, and she was quite certain Kyle had dyslexia.

In fact, at one point during his weekly vision therapy session, this experienced clinician stated, "I would eat my dog if Kyle doesn't have dyslexia."

Although research has stated that dyslexia isn't associated with eye problems, the visual motor skills Kyle gained helped him tremendously with his classroom activities, and with hockey.

Vision is a primary tool through which traditional learning takes place. When a child uses both eyes in unity, then he or she can maintain clarity easily and without visual stress. He or she is then able to devote much more of his or her energy and attention to the acquisition of meaning and to the academic task at hand. This is true visual attention.

On the other hand, daydreaming, inattention, and acting out are all possible consequences of the visual stress that a child may experience when he or she cannot scan words on a page, or maintain clarity of the print.

This stress interferes tremendously with the ability to learn easily and efficiently.

If a child is compensating for any other learning difficulty, the visual skill inefficiencies will greatly compound the problem.

My gifted little boy was not only dealing with dyslexia, he was also having difficulty with visual efficiency and visual information processing. To make matters worse, Kyle also had an inexperienced first grade teacher. It was just her first year teaching first grade, and only her second year teaching overall.

However, with all of this going on, my primary responsibility was keeping my son confident and building his self esteem at every opportunity.

It is important to note that dyslexia is also associated with auditory discrimination skills, or lack thereof. Auditory discrimination allows people to hear and accurately process what is being said.

People who have dyslexia sometimes cannot discriminate the words they hear as well as other people can. For example one night at the dinner table I said to my younger son Liam, "You have to practice your states after dinner," and my older son Kyle said, "What, I have to sharpen my skates after dinner?" Kyle has difficulty with auditory discrimination at times, and this only compounds other problems caused by dyslexia.

Like many youngsters, Kyle also hated homework! He would often cry, and tell me that his brain was tired. He would say, "I hate words, they mix up my brain." He also would say that sometimes in class, "I have a white out. My brain just goes blank." Here is my little boy explaining how his working memory is not serving him well.

It was heart-wrenching!

But I would reassure him, and tell him that that happens to me, and that I have to write lists every day of my life to keep up.

I also told him how very smart, nice and talented he was—daily. We asked his first grade teacher to PLEASE do the same, but unfortunately she did not.

**First Eligibility Meeting**

After most of the CORE testing was complete, we had our first eligibility meeting to determine if Kyle was eligible for an Individualized Educational Plan (IEP). These plans are often of great necessity to learning disabled children.

One of the reasons we believed Kyle was eligible for an IEP was that the CORE evaluation found that Kyle had significant learning issues—scoring well below average in such areas as reading, writing, math and auditory processing.

Moreover, these learning problems prevented Kyle from progressing effectively in the general education program without specially designed instruction.

In spite of the public school district's own testing results, our town found my son Kyle "not eligible' for Special Education services under an IEP plan, because according to them, Kyle did not have any learning disabilities.

How could this be so?

Because, according to the public school staff, he did not have a learning disability that warranted an IEP plan.

The public school staff on Kyle's first eligibility team recommended continued regular educational supports consisting of working with the reading specialist three times per week. Kyle's first eligibility team—except for his parents, of course—found he did not meet the criteria for an IEP.

Nothing could be further from the truth. I adamantly disagreed with the team, and pleaded at this first eligibility meeting for an IEP for Kyle.

I stated there was a strong family history of dyslexia, and that their own testing showed Kyle had learning disabilities.

For these reasons and others, we strongly believed Kyle was in need of specialized instruction. This plea fell on deaf ears.

The public school staff said they would monitor Kyle's progress. My natural curiosity had me wondering "Who is going to monitor this progress, and by what standards? If this monitoring did not occur, what would be the consequences?"

The public school district notified us of their decision to deny an IEP for Kyle on or about March 4, 1994.

However, the school district also found that Kyle was having difficulty with the new math program, which was language based. Unbelievably, they still did not find Kyle eligible for Special Education services. Instead, they had him work with the regular education tutor two times per week for 15 minutes during math time.

Curiously, all Kyle's supports were regular education versus Special Education—which is what he desperately needed.

Special Education allows children similar to Kyle to have specialized instruction, enabling them to access the curriculum with an IEP—and truly make effective progress.

Due to Kyle's dyslexia, it was imperative he receive specialized instruction that included a lower adult-pupil ratio, an individually designed curriculum, and all the necessary therapies. But he was getting none of this.

As a result of the school district's "finding of no eligibility"—in spite of the results of their own evaluation—we procured an independent evaluation.

Dr. Chase, a respected neuropsychologist, conducted this neuropsychological evaluation on March 17, 19 and 27, 1994.

As is detailed later in this chapter, Dr. Chase confirmed that Kyle did in fact have learning disabilities.

During this time frame, I also requested to meet with the Head of Special Education, Mr. Grady, to plead with him for an IEP for Kyle. This meeting took place shortly after the first eligibility meeting, and this is what happened.

## Meeting With Head of Special Education

We requested to meet with Mr. Grady, who was the Head of Special Education. He acted as if he knew what was best for my son Kyle, and insisted we simply "go along" with the eligibility team's recommendation. Or at least that was my impression.

During our meeting, I discussed the need for Kyle to have an IEP due to his disability. I stated that the CORE testing indicated that Kyle was in need of an IEP, and that there was a strong family history of dyslexia.

I also asked if there was anything Mr. Grady could do to try and facilitate Kyle's IEP—or if there was any way he could persuade the team to reevaluate their decision to deny. However, early on in this meeting, I realized that he was not going to ask the team to reconsider. Later on in this book, the reader will see I was correct with this assumption.

Mr. Grady told me there was a process in place, and he gave me a copy of a book written by Sally Shaywitz, M.D., which I referenced earlier in this book. I read the book, gained a great deal of knowledge from it, and returned the book to Mr. Grady at a later date with a "Thank You" card.

Mr. Grady told me that a strong phonics-based curriculum is what Dr. Shaywitz recommends for children who have dyslexia, and he said our town has just implemented a Wilson Fundations phonics-based curriculum in the first and second grades. Mr. Grady also said Kyle was receiving this curriculum as part of regular education, not Special Education.

Although the Fundations program was a phonics-based program, it was not a scientifically proven program that children with dyslexia, like Kyle, desperately need (something Dr. Shaywitz recommends in her book).

I wondered, did Mr. Grady even read the book, Overcoming Dyslexia written by Dr. Shaywitz? Or was he just passing out copies of her book to desperate parents?

I told Mr. Grady that Kyle was crying before school, and that he was upset about going to school. Mr. Grady's initial response was, "What kid wouldn't rather be playing—versus going to school?"

I stated there is a difference between not wanting to go to school, and fearing school. I also stated that Kyle is in first grade and should be "skipping to school." Mr. Grady then shared that he himself was dyslexic, and that he would not want to see a child suffer. Mr. Grady also said that he had worked with Barbara Wilson, who developed the curriculum our town was currently using.

At this point, I informed Mr. Grady that I would be getting independent testing for Kyle. One reason for this decision was that I felt as though the first eligibility team members did not objectively analyze their data, and I was quite certain my son Kyle had dyslexia. In addition, my family history alerted me to the fact that I should get independent testing.

This second neuropsychologist, Dr. Chase, also observed and tested Kyle. The only difference between this neuropsychologist, and the first one, was that I was paying for the comprehensive evaluations of the second doctor. More importantly, I would be getting her results in writing.

Mr. Grady then told me that I was a great advocate, so in his opinion, I did not even need an educational advocate, which thankfully I had already hired. My educational advocate's name was Ms. Greer. Being the youngest of nine children, and watching some of my older sisters advocate for my nieces and nephews who had learning disabilities, prepared me early on as to the importance of hiring a qualified educational advocate.

Thankfully, I didn't fall for Mr. Grady's complimentary advice, about serving as Kyle's educational advocate myself.

I believe this advice was given to me because Mr. Grady realized that it would be almost impossible for a working parent to learn and comprehend all the various Federal and State Laws and rules and regulations surrounding my son's educational and due process rights.

I ask you, how is a parent supposed to work full time, advocate full time for Special Education services, drive two children to sporting events, conduct special interventions, complete homework and special projects, cook dinner, and do laundry—all while competently navigating the procedural guidelines and education laws of the state and federal governments?

I don't know, but it seems a little odd this would even be expected of a parent. One would think there would be more help available to parents who only want to do what is right.

Because I was getting nowhere fast, I also hired a Special Education attorney at this time. My attorney's name was Margaret.

I stressed before leaving Mr. Grady's office that I appreciated everything being done for my son Kyle. At the same time, I let Mr. Grady know that I knew Kyle had significant learning disabilities and needed Special Education and specialized instruction.

Then, I thanked him for his time and left his office.

### Neuropsychological Testing With Dr. Chase

A few weeks later, following our meeting with Mr. Grady, Kyle participated in three days of neuropsychological testing. This testing was hard for Kyle. After he completed it he said, "It's like I have a factory of men working in my brain and it worked so hard that my brain exploded and now I have to rebuild it."

Dr. Chase's evaluation confirmed the results of the school testing that Kyle did in fact have learning disabilities that prevented him from making effective progress without specially designed instruction. She also noted that Kyle had average-to-very superior intelligence in her report.

In addition, during the neuropsychological testing with Dr. Chase, she made a number of comments about my son Kyle.

Although it is difficult to write about these comments, I want to share this information in the hope that parents realize the importance of independent testing.

Kyle reported to Dr. Chase that he experiences difficulty in his "brain" when he struggled on school tasks, and that he has concerns about getting "in trouble" because of his difficulties. Kyle openly complained about the physical reactions he experienced in his "brain" that seemed related to overload.

During one test, which included oral direction and visual display that instructed Kyle to scan for diamonds, and then circle them, Kyle asked, "You mean the cube?"

Dr. Chase said, "No, the diamond!"

Kyle then proceeded to color-in a triangle shape, instead of circling it. During the testing, Kyle also produced two basic elements from the beginning of the story and commented, "The other parts got emptied out of my brain. It got erased."

It was painful to see that Kyle understood the difficulty he was having was excessive. He said, "This shouldn't be so hard."

On another test, Kyle made statements such as "No idea!" "That's really tough." or "I can't do it!" when he was asked to generate guesses to answer questions he had left blank.

On one basic concept, after Kyle earned partial credit for using a word in a sentence, he stated, "I don't really know. Don't know how to explain. Hardly know anything about it."

Kyle's complaints about his difficulties included statements indicative of an overload reaction, as he reported, "Just can't think of anything else. My brain is running out of juice."

On the pre-primer Kyle read, "He sawed saw to car" instead of "He started to cry." Ironically this quote, and the information above, are reflective of my son's early struggles with his dyslexia.

In addition, Kyle's private reading tutor, who had been working with my son on a weekly basis since the winter of 1992, conducted an independent reading test with Kyle.

These results also showed that Kyle had disabilities, and that he was not making effective progress. Kyle liked his reading tutor, but it was not always easy to get him to go to the tutor. We had some tears before some sessions, and Kyle would share with me that his reading tutor "gives me too many words."

## Second Eligibility Meeting

As stated previously, I sought assistance from an educational advocate because the task of advocating for an IEP is so overwhelming for a working parent—or anyone not trained to accomplish this task, for that matter.

My educational advocate, Ms. Greer, was very helpful during this process.

Moving forward, a second eligibility meeting occurred on April 10, 1994. Dr. Chase, our private neuropsychologist, and Ms. Greer, our private educational advocate, were also present at the second eligibility meeting, at our expense.

Unbelievably, their combined hourly rate was more than our food budget for a family of four for the month!

Even with the new documented testing results that included a confirmed diagnosis of dyslexia, our efforts were to no avail as the school reaffirmed their position of "no eligibility" for an IEP for Kyle.

How could this be happening?

I have been an OT for approximately 22 years, and I've worked with various people with different disabilities. I've always reviewed the data, and then, I made appropriate recommendations based on that data.

I started to think, "Maybe I'm crazy. The school is informing me that Kyle is just fine, and that he is making effective progress, but at home I am observing the contrary—and experienced independent evaluators are observing and reporting significant disabilities."

I also started to think, "Could it be the cost associated with specialized instruction? Or the recognition that the school district did not have an appropriate language-based learning program to meet my son's learning needs? Or could it be the potential cost associated with a private placement?"

Prior to the second eligibility meeting, our educational advocate, Ms. Greer, sent the neuropsychologist's (Dr. Chase's) private testing evaluation via certified mail to the Head of Special Education, Mr. Grady.

Ms. Greer also requested, in writing, that Mr. Grady deliver the private testing evaluation to the members of Kyle's eligibility team prior to the second eligibility meeting.

This written request was made approximately 12 days prior to the second eligibility meeting. This gave Mr. Grady ample opportunity to pass this important information to his subordinates, the eligibility team members, or at least delegate this task to the Principal, Mr. Davis. After all, Mr. Grady was the Head of Special Education. Therefore, one would hope that he knew this was his responsibility, and the importance of it in the life of a child.

This "pass on" of the testing results was critical to helping the eligibility team members' review, and hopefully, would confirm the need for my son to receive specialized services. In this way, Kyle could finally access the curriculum he so desperately needed.

Unfortunately for all involved, Mr. Grady never delivered the evaluation, as requested in writing.

I learned this fact early in the same day that the second eligibility meeting was scheduled.

Therefore, I had to hand-deliver the evaluations to all the members of Kyle's team that morning...and the meeting was scheduled for that afternoon!

This is just one of the many procedural violations that occurred during this process.

The requirements regarding Special Education are based on State and Federal Law. The relevant laws are the following:

State Law: The state Special Education law, popularly known as "Chapter 766" after the session law number under which it was passed in 1972, is contained in the Massachusetts General Laws (MGL) at Chapter 71B. The regulations implementing the statute are found in the Code of Massachusetts Regulations (CMR) at 603 CMR, Section 28.00.

Federal Law: The federal Special Education law is known as "IDEA" (Individuals with Disabilities Education Act). The statute is located in the United States Code at 20 U.S.C. Sec. 1400. In 2004, Congress reauthorized the IDEA and the amended statute is popularly referred to as "IDEA-2004." The implementing regulations for IDEA will be found in the Code of Federal Regulations (CFR) at Chapter 34, Section 300.

> (As adopted from Notice of Procedural Safeguards, formerly known as the "Parents Rights Brochure.")

I have learned that eligibility team members should be given private testing results approximately 10 days prior to an eligibility meeting. Because of this and other, in my opinion, "deny and delay" incidents, the IEP process was agonizing at times.

Although I must admit, Ms. Connors, Kyle's public school teacher, did notice his gift with art. I am thankful for that.

Even so, Ms. Connors once said to me, at the end of a very long and frustrating first grade year, "Well, if Kyle ever wants to make money, he can sell his art work on the street."

Was this her way of giving a compliment? I'm not really sure. But it sure did not feel like a compliment at the time.

Due to the long and arduous process that was still going on related to my son's Special Education needs and the school staff's inappropriate responses, I was feeling upset. My son's daily struggles and my frustration with the school and their response were constant.

When Ms. Connors made that comment, I wanted to respond by saying, "Yes he could, but it would also be nice if he could read and write," but I didn't. I bit my lip and smiled.

In addition to the pursuit of an IEP for Kyle, there was also a discussion of a 504 Plan. (Please note Kyle had already been on such a plan three-and-a-half years previously—which might be one clue as to why he needed an IEP versus another 504.)

Unlike the Individuals Disabilities Education Act (IDEA), Section 504 does not require that a student with a disability have a detailed Individual Education Plan (IEP).

If a child is eligible for Special Education under the IDEA Act, which we and many other competent professionals STRONGLY believed Kyle was, of course he must have an IEP.

The Individual Education Plan is a legal binding document. Kyle qualified for an IEP for two reasons according to the law.

First, he had a Specific Learning Disability, which includes, by definition, dyslexia.

Second, he was unable to progress effectively in regular education as a result of his disability.

Approximately one week after the second eligibility meeting, Kyle's teacher informed me that there was a "note" in Kyle's backpack that turned out to be a draft 504 Plan. The plan detailed difficulties Kyle was having in the area of sensory integration, basic reading and written expression.

Recommendations in these areas were outlined. However, this 504 Plan was not calculated to meet Kyle's learning needs, based on my explanation in the previous paragraphs.

Not only was it my professional opinion that Kyle was entitled to an IEP, but it was also the professional opinion of a second neuropsychologist, Dr. Chase, who evaluated my son. Later on, a third neuropsychologist, Dr. Ellen, also confirmed the diagnosis of dyslexia.

Moreover, Kyle's private 1:1 reading tutor, his developmental optometrist, and his occupational therapist all agreed that Kyle was in need of an IEP.

Finally, I found it shocking—not to mention poor decision making—for a special educator to put a 504 Plan in the backpack of a child who struggles tremendously with organization.

## Third Eligibility Meeting

Two weeks later the team reconvened. This was the third eligibility meeting and I still—naïve as it may sound—believed that Kyle's eligibility team members would finally agree that my young son was in need of an IEP.

At the start of the meeting, I had the following prepared statement to help me begin what turned out to be another disappointing meeting:

*"There are no dictators in this room—only leaders in education and I am one of them. Being a parent, it is not always easy to sit in these meetings and remain cool, calm and collected, but I am doing my best. After reviewing*

*approximately 21 evaluations administered with our son
Kyle, starting with the most recent and going back to when
he was approximately four years old, it is clear to me that he
has significant learning disabilities.*

*Because all of you have been given these reports in writing,
and have administered some of them—and we have sat in
two eligibility meetings together without a consensus for an
Individualized Educational Plan (IEP)—I thought perhaps by
hearing some of the significant findings, Kyle's IEP team will
acknowledge that he has significant learning disabilities and is in
need of an IEP.*

*I am going to start with the most recent testing and go
backward to show significant findings to emphasize his need
for individualized services and show all of the interventions
he has received thus far."*

At this meeting I pleaded with the team to give Kyle an
IEP and summer services, but they said no.

The public school continued to hold the position that Kyle
was making effective progress, but that they would forward
a second draft of the 504 Plan because "his parents" were
expressing concerns about Kyle's frustration.

This statement was actually infuriating, because Kyle
himself was expressing his frustration to anyone who
would listen.

In spite of numerous school and independent testing results—and with a complete disregard for Kyle's own words to the various evaluators—the eligibility team members continued to deny Kyle an appropriate IEP, and stated that only his parents were expressing concerns. The insinuation is that "his parents" were the only ones concerned about and experiencing Kyle's frustration. I don't think so!

The therapists, school psychologist, and teachers documented his frustrations—and the Principal, Mr. Davis, was going to lay this on me as a mother?

To reiterate: I don't think so!

The public school speech and language pathologist discharged Kyle from speech and language three years earlier due to his "frustration level" in writing.

The public school psychologist documented that Kyle said, "I hate spelling, I am extremely bad at minuses. They are too hard for me." She also stated in her report that Kyle appears to know that he is not strong academically.

The Special Education teacher who administered the academic test for the CORE wrote in her report that, when Kyle was asked why he did not like writing, Kyle responded "Too much writing gets my head mixed up."

When Kyle met with her again, she documented, "As for the second session, Kyle was happy to discover that there would be no writing, and he would be beginning with math. He asked if he could have a number grid for completing math items. He was told that he would have to try it without it first. This seemed to frustrate Kyle."

After this incident, Kyle was quicker to say, "I can't do this," and could not always be persuaded to try.

During this second session with the Special Education teacher, Kyle was given a picture of a child's birthday party. He wrote "It was the boy's birthday." When asked by the evaluator if he could add some more, Kyle said that he did not have anything else to add.

When the examiner offered to do the physical writing for him my son added, "And he got a present and everyone tried to whack the piñata open."

I included this vignette to help clarify for the reader that when my son did not have to complete the physical writing, he was willing and able to continue with the story. Due to the severity of his dyslexia, reading and writing were very difficult for him.

From some of the interactions illustrated above, one can clearly see how my son's frustration was being voiced to all that would listen. What is going on? The school district wants to paint me out to be the only one hearing a little boy's frustrations with learning due to his obvious—at least to me—disabilities.

The IEP process is also emotionally and financially draining on a family. During my meetings with the school district, I often stated that I wished what they were saying was correct. I wanted my son's testing to come back verifying that he had no learning disabilities.

The simple truth is this: All the testing by the school and the independent evaluations dramatically showed Kyle has dyslexia—and in need of specialized instruction in order for him to make truly "effective progress."

Moreover, the emotional and financial burden placed on a family to undertake this "David vs. Goliath" struggle simply encourages the school district to "deny and delay," in my opinion.

The school district knows all this full well, and they understand the expense of sending a child who has dyslexia to a private school, and/or the expense associated with providing him or her with an IEP and specialized instruction. I wonder how many parents simply accept the school's word. And how many can't afford the fight?

I also used to wonder, "Has the district read its own reports?"

I would leave the eligibility meetings shaking my head and asking, "How can they observe my son's struggles, document his learning disabilities, write such things as 'he seems to know he struggles academically'—and then say he only expresses frustration about learning at home?"

Moreover, how can they simply dismiss Kyle's learning disabilities, their own CORE testing, independent evaluations, family history, and the parents' observations and concerns?

I often wondered why they would deny my son the appropriate educational services. I have come to the realization that the school district understands that this "process" is long, arduous, and a very expensive endeavor.

Perhaps the problem might just "go away"...

This realization led to more and more questions.

How many parents don't have the money to pay for independent testing?

How many parents can't afford an advocate, so they never learn about their child's legal/educational rights?

How many parents who have the money simply leave the public school system and don't hold the public school district responsible and accountable for providing the "free and appropriate education" their child is entitled to, as stated under the law?

How many children never receive the educational services they are entitled to overall?

The IEP process is clearly overwhelming; however, I believe it is imperative that each child receive an appropriate education.

I also believe that parents, whenever possible, should follow the process—so that the school district's unwritten policy of "deny and delay," in my opinion, is exposed.

The only part that made this whole process a little more bearable was watching Kyle complete his artwork, and seeing his sense of accomplishment.

Language-based learning disabilities are indicative of difficulties in the left side of the brain, which is the primary language area. Many people with dyslexia are incredibly artistic due to this difference in the wiring of the brain. One of the functions for the right side of the brain is creativity.

Despite this brief respite, the IEP process continued unabated.

Due to time constraints, I advised the public school in writing on June 4, 1994, that I was placing Kyle at

The Carroll School, a private school designed to treat bright children with language-based learning disabilities. It is interesting to note that my educational advocate informed me that I had to notify the public school in writing—and specify the time frame. Imagine if I took Mr. Grady's compliment and advice to act as my son's educational advocate myself. I may not have known this critical fact! How could I have?

Failure on my part to properly provide the public school district with this information would have resulted in a violation—and may very well have prevented me from pursuing my son's "due process" rights to a free and appropriate education under the law.

A "free and appropriate" education—as defined by the Individuals with Disabilities Education Act of 2004 (Enrolled as Agreed to or Passed by Both House and Senate in the United States of America Sec. 602)—means the Special Educations of children like Kyle:

(A) must have been provided at public expense, under public supervision and direction, and without charge;

(B) meet the standards of the state educational agency;

(C) include an appropriate pre-school, elementary school, or secondary school education in the state involved; and

(D) are provided in conformity with the individualized education program required under section 614 (d).

(Resource, H. R. 1350)

It is imperative that parents understand the laws, as well as their obligations as parents.

Although the word "free" is used in the law, one must consider that we pay a considerable amount of money in taxes, which helps pay for education, public school administrator salaries, teacher salaries, professional development, curriculum design, etc.

Moreover, at the end of the day, this is the law. This is what I want for my son Kyle, because he is entitled to it. No more no less. Just as I would advocate for any child who has Special Education needs. I did not create the law, but as a taxpayer and advocate for my learning disabled son, Kyle, I will do my level best to make sure it is upheld.

On another note, dyslexia in some ways is easier to ignore, because it is a hidden disability.

For example, it is more difficult to ignore a child in a wheelchair or a child who is hearing or visually impaired.

Now it's back to the IEP process. At this point, I requested that the public school system pay for the outside placement of my son. After all, there was significant evidence that Kyle had a disability and he was NOT making effective progress.

The school district, however, continued to maintain that Kyle was making effective progress, and therefore was not eligible for Special Education services. In addition, the school district refused to honor my request for reimbursement.

The good news is that with my perseverance, and the guidance of an experienced educational advocate and Special Education attorney, the process continued. Moreover, we learned there would be a neutral party charged with examining all of the evaluations, assessments and observations. If and when a hearing was held, this party would make a decision based on the law and the evidence. Halleluiah!

At this point, the public school sent a revised draft of the 504 Plan to me, because they had denied the IEP again. It was June 7, 1994. The plan would be for the following year.

The public school Principal, Mr. Davis, indicated that based on their assessment, Kyle did not have a disability in math, so math was no longer considered in this new 504 Plan.

He did recommend that Kyle begin the school year with a regular education tutor in math.

However, Dr. Chase, a respected neuropsychologist, documented in her evaluation the following:

"Kyle showed vulnerabilities to difficulties with math performance within the instructional format and requirements for showing knowledge typical in a school setting, and functioning was well below expectations for his intellectual abilities, consistent with a disorder in math."

The effect of this action, and the new 504 Plan, was actually taking math services away—from a plan that was not sufficient in the first place to meet Kyle's unique learning needs!

Meanwhile, my son Kyle had been working with a math tutor since the prior winter. So Kyle has needed a math tutor in first grade—and he will need one in second grade because he has been diagnosed with a disorder in math—but it is no longer necessary to put math in his proposed 504 Plan?

I ask you, does this make sense?

Finally, Mr. Davis proposed another team meeting for the second week in September. This meeting never occurred.

It is no wonder children fall so far behind so fast with this type of incompetence (in my professional and personal opinion).

There is nothing more parents want to hear than their child is doing just fine, and he or she is making effective progress. But are they really? This is the important and difficult question that must be asked.

During the summer of 1994, I continued to advocate for my son Kyle. We did pursue mediation in an attempt to resolve our disputes.

## The Mediation Process

A mediation session was held on July 11, 1994, before a state appointed mediator from the Department of Education. Unfortunately, no resolution was reached, and my son Kyle started second grade at The Carroll School, a private school, which services bright children with dyslexia.

During mediation, the public school administrator and the parents are supposed to present their positions. The mediator then meets with each side privately in the hopes that a mutually satisfying agreement can be reached between the two parties. As stated above, no resolution was reached at the mediation.

However, our educational advocate found the mediator's words encouraging, and she decided it was best to convey this information to our attorney.

Even so, the public school head of Special Education made absolutely no change to the initial denial of an IEP. Following this mediation, we wondered, "Is this just one more way the school district gets to 'deny and delay' services for Kyle?" At least, this was our impression.

And we thought, "Is this one more way to run up our out-of-pocket expenses, one more way to frustrate us in the process—hoping that we would give up and go away?"

Prior to all of the meetings I have documented, I spent hours compiling, summarizing and preparing presentations to advocate for my son to receive an IEP and an appropriate education, with no luck to this point.

Also, due to a significant back injury, I couldn't just go out and run three miles as I frequently did in the past to relieve my stress. So I found myself, more and more, working on this book to tell our story to help others deal with this type of situation should it occur with other children.

I believe it is abundantly clear that the process, as it exists today, is stacked against the individual student and his or her parents who are challenging the system. Therefore, it is my hope this book provides some help.

This process is so long and disturbing one has to keep a sense of humor. One has to laugh at times or as a parent you will not survive this agonizing process.

In any event, I now realize I will be pursuing our son's due process right to a hearing concerning his educational needs and rights. We did have a meeting that summer or early fall with our wonderful educational advocate, and our superb Special Education attorney, to review our actions to date and plan for future actions.

I compiled 14 different documents of evidence showing that my son has significant learning disabilities, including dyslexia.

Finally, when I delivered all of this information to my Special Education attorney, I felt a lighter load. It was reassuring to know that someone who cared about the law and children was going to review these materials and help advocate for my son Kyle! This was a good feeling.

But life has a funny way of knocking us back down. When I was driving back from the meeting with our Special Education attorney and educational advocate, just as I arrived in my hometown, my car broke down!

Not only was I looking at paying an extraordinary amount of money for an appropriate educational environment for my son, I also was going to be responsible for a $3,000 bill for a new transmission. How does the saying go? When it rains, it pours!

Oh well, at least I knew my son's disabilities were going to be addressed, and I had a magnificent attorney who was helping me advocate for him.

Artist: Kyle, Age 8

# Chapter 4

"I was, on the whole, considerably
discouraged by my schooldays.
It was not pleasant to feel oneself
so completely outclassed and
left behind at the beginning of the race."

**Winston Churchill**

# Second Grade

At the end of the first day at The Carroll School Kyle jumped in the car and said, "This is the best school."

This was a welcome change from our long and difficult days from the previous year. Before bed that night he said, "Mommy, do you know what?" And I said "No, what?" He said, "I have the best teacher in the whole world."

I'll never forget that day as long as I live, and you know what? I bet Kyle won't either.

We believe that his second grade teacher changed Kyle's life in the most positive way, and we are forever grateful.

In the middle of his second grade experience, our attorney advised us that it would be beneficial if Kyle underwent a second independent neuropsychological evaluation with Dr. Ellen. I write "second" here because although this is Kyle's third meeting with a neuropsychologist, it will be the second meeting where we would be paying for the evaluation, and all the findings would be in writing.

Although I was hesitant to put Kyle through more testing, I did want to see that he was benefiting from his new school, so I conceded. Also, it is beneficial to have this data to assist your learning disabled youngster.

Consistent with all prior testing, including the CORE evaluation, Dr. Ellen found that Kyle did in fact suffer from language-based learning disabilities, a reading disorder, a disorder of written language, and executive functioning learning disabilities (dyslexia).

Dr. Ellen made a number of specific recommendations, but most importantly felt that Kyle needed a highly structured language-based program.

It should be noted that Dr. Ellen's evaluation of Kyle occurred after he had been enrolled at The Carroll School, which teaches students with dyslexia, for several months. Therefore, the testing revealed that Kyle had shown immense improvement, particularly with his reading.

However, Dr. Ellen cautioned that while Kyle's skills were emerging, he still needed direct instruction in a small setting with teachers trained and certified in working with language-based, learning disabled students.

Ms. Greer forwarded Dr. Ellen's report to the public elementary school and requested a meeting to review and discuss the report. The report was sent to Mr. Grady, Head of Special Education on April 18, 1995. Mr. Grady responded by stating that the eligibility process would start anew and sent a "Consent to Evaluate" (CORE) form to me.

However, we were not seeking to initiate a new CORE evaluation.

We were requesting a continuation of the IEP process, whereby Dr. Ellen's evaluation would be reviewed by the public school's eligibility team, and we were entitled to this consideration of new facts based on the law.

It was our hope that the public school eligibility staff would FINALLY provide our son with an appropriate IEP, which was needed and reported on in all the public and private testing.

I refused to consent to further evaluation, because we believed it was not necessary, and ample testing had already been administered. We thought this was one more way to deny and delay the process.

Shortly thereafter, our attorney forwarded a demand letter to Mr. Grady in another attempt to resolve these issues. This attempt went unrecognized, and we proceeded with the process.

## Fourth Eligibility Meeting

Contact was made between our attorney and the school's attorney, and a meeting was held on August 21, 1995, to consider Dr. Ellen's report, which is required by law.

Once again, the public school reiterated their position of "no eligibility." Subsequent to this meeting, the school made a nominal monetary offer to our attorney to resolve this dispute.

In our opinion, the offer was not made in good faith. It did not even equal the per pupil expenditure of a regular education student for one year in our school district.

At no point did they ever offer any individualized special education interventions, which Kyle desperately required, and continues to require based on his learning disabilities.

I rejected the offer, and began the process of filing a hearing request with my attorney. The fact that the school made a nominal monetary offer, while still maintaining "no eligibility," was surprising. If they thought they were in the right, why offer money?

However, because the offer was so minimal, and because we had spent an exorbitant amount of money, we decided to proceed to a hearing.

Based on the totality of all of Kyle's testing, the actions of the Special Education director seemed unconscionable. How could he possibly contend in the August 1995 meeting that my son did not have a language-based learning disability?

How dare he make this statement, when he is not qualified to do so! Was this his attempt to show his superiority, loud and clear, in front of his staff as he blatantly dismissed the diagnoses from two trained professionals?

This declaration came in spite of my son being accepted to a top school in the United States that services ONLY children with language-based learning disabilities; diagnoses from two neuropsychologists; evaluations from two reading specialists; and the public school's eligibility team members own Special Education testing—all of which clearly show Kyle's disabilities.

And I ask, if this was the public school's position, why bother to have this meeting at all? It cost us more money, frustration, and simply delayed a hearing.

Well, the reassuring thought at this time is that a neutral hearings officer may disagree with Mr. Grady.

While all this was going on, Kyle continued to progress nicely in his new school. After receiving the appropriate education, he is much more confident. One of his teachers recently said he came up to her and proudly said, "I'm no longer dyslexic in reading. I'm only dyslexic in math now."

Another cute anecdote is one night while my two boys were doing their homework, my younger son Liam, who is in regular education, and was working on a difficult abstract multi-step language-based math problem. But he did not come up with an easy answer as quickly as usual.

My son Kyle was quick to pick up on his younger brother's difficulty, and whispered to me, "I know the answer to that. Are you sure he doesn't have dyslexia?"

I thought, "Oh Lord I hope not!"

The power of empowering a young child cannot be underestimated! My son Kyle was so proud at that moment that he had the correct answer quicker than his little brother.

Another incident occurred when Liam was working very hard on some difficult math word problems. Kyle walked by and said, "Oh wow, we don't have hard homework like that at my school. Is Liam really doing those hard numbers?"

A different incident occurred recently. Kyle and Liam were with me and Kyle asked, "Do all your sisters have dyslexia or just some of them?" I answered "I have dyslexia, and a couple my sisters have dyslexia."

If I was guessing, I'd say my sister, who has a daughter diagnosed with dyslexia—and myself, who has a son diagnosed with dyslexia—both have dyslexia.

Are we noticing that pattern again?

Next, my son Kyle asked, "Are there dyslexic colleges?" I responded stating, "Yes there are!" Kyle then said, "I am worried. What happens if I go to the Diamond Middle School (which is the public school in our home town) and it is too hard? If this happens, can I go back to my school I am in now?"

He then said, "I don't know how to do the big numbers like 1 million plus 500 plus 63." I told him not to worry and we would always make good decisions about his schooling. His little brother was proud of the fact that he knew the answer to his brother's concern and piped up, "Kyle, do not worry. That is not too hard. It would be one million, five hundred and sixty-three." I told them I loved them and it was time to go to sleep.

It has been a long road with many dark days; however, my son Kyle was beginning to realize that college was an option for him. The fact that he was asking about dyslexic colleges was great, because he felt good about learning in a safe environment. His confidence with school is growing, although he still expresses concerns about returning to public middle school.

I believe this reluctance, and his lack of confidence, are a direct result of a disastrous first grade experience.

Kyle is a very sensitive child who is aware that school does not come easily to him. However, he is learning beneficial strategies to assist him with his learning for the rest of his life.

As far as my own experience with dyslexia, it is a constant battle. I'm sure it differs for each individual. At times, I get this feeling within me like I am going to forget something mid-sentence, which is very frustrating.

Another difficulty that Kyle and I share happens when we're playing a game where someone is describing a movie or character. This is a game Kyle, Liam and his cousins played during the summer, and once in a while, adults would join in.

Consistently, Kyle would never guess the right answer, and eventually would drop out of the game. My guesses would always be wrong. Or, I would be able to picture the person or movie scene in my head—but I just would not be able to come up with the name. This is sooooooo frustrating!

Kyle did not like these games, and he would often choose not to play when the kids started. I have to admit that I didn't blame him, because I experienced his frustration and I am a grown adult.

One more difficulty I experience is that I'll be sitting with a group of friends, and we will be discussing a topic. While I am formulating my thoughts to contribute to the conversation, the topic has changed.

This happens to Kyle as well, but he has learned to speak up at the dinner table and say, "I have something to say and I have to say it now or I'll forget it!" He states this adamantly, in sometimes a panicked and frustrated tone. Liam also gets upset when he is talking and gets interrupted like this, but he usually goes directly back to his story with ease.

This is just part of our life.

Spending time with my sisters and watching them process information has been fascinating because of all the knowledge I now have about dyslexia.

All of my sisters are wonderful, loving people who suffer from some processing issues, in my professional opinion. Interestingly, it does not seem to bother them, except for one, like it does me.

This is not to say it is not frustrating for them sometimes trying to figure out directions for the first time, or being put in a foreign situation without much preparation. There are numerous times I have spoken to my sisters where they were lost and frustrated with directions. But they seem to handle it and get from point A to point B.

Many of them just accept this is just who they are. I must admit together we are great problem solvers. Because we process information similarly, we can get together and have several conversations going on at once. This seems normal to us, but for others they just shake their heads in disbelief that we can keep track of all the different stories.

My sisters and I have the ability to multitask. Through our life experiences, we have learned that advocacy, tenacity, and hard work go a long way in reaching our goals.

It is directly because of my achievements, educationally and professionally, that I am able to pay for my son to be in an appropriate learning environment—while doggedly pursuing my son's due process rights to a "free and appropriate education" as guaranteed to him by Federal and State Laws.

As a tax-paying citizen, I have as much right as anyone else to a public education for my children under the law. As long as Kyle is entitled to Special Education services, I will continue to advocate for the appropriate education and protect his rights. It is my hope that all parents will do the same and seek appropriate services to help their child with dyslexia.

Artist: Kyle, Age 9

# Chapter 5

"Under IDEA school districts must create an individualized education program for each disabled child."

**Supreme Court Justice Sandra Day O'Connor**

# The Process

The process is ongoing. And I find myself checking E-mails every opportunity I get. My mind is always going.

What if Kyle needs years of specialized instruction?

What if we can't pay for it?

What if Kyle gets anxiety about transitioning back?

What if? What if? What if?

I'm so tired of living this way.

I find myself checking the Bureau of Special Education Appeals (BSEA) rulings and learning how hearings officers come to their decisions in similar cases.

What if they think Kyle was too young to be diagnosed as dyslexic? I know that the research is out there to the contrary, but has the hearings officer read the research?

What if he has not?

My conversations with significant others are dominated by the struggles of my son Kyle and his educational needs. People are getting tired of listening, but as a parent I have this need to be advocating, to be helping, to be assisting others.

This whole process is happening for a reason. I'm not quite sure why, but I will hopefully one day understand it.

Any negative situation can be turned positive; therefore, the purpose of this book is to educate and help others. Everyone in this world needs support.

I'm also angry. I'm angry that public school districts do not have enough money, and/or that they do not allocate what they have properly to service children with learning disabilities. I'm angry that public school districts seemingly look the other way, and refuse to acknowledge dyslexia, because of the price tag associated with it.

Multidisciplinary evaluations administered in schools can be very helpful, but I believe they are susceptible to biases and conflicts of interest. School budgeting constraints or lack of personnel may also affect the quality of evaluations and the extent of recommended services.

Also, one must realize that conducting the testing is only the first step. If the representatives of the public school staff refuse to objectively analyze their own data, their own testing is rendered utterly useless.

Due to these limitations, independent evaluations for a second opinion are imperative in cases like my son Kyle's.

Instead of spending time and money to try and avoid accountability, why not spend time and money on researching the effective programs? Why not try to reduce class sizes?

Why not start language-based learning programs with scientifically proven methods in first grade, instead of waiting until a child falls two or three years behind?

Why let children feel bad about themselves, and struggle to get up every day and go into a classroom where very little makes sense?

I'm angry that I have to spend vacation days preparing for a case, because educators refused to give my son an IEP and appropriately address his disabilities!

I have never been an angry person, so this is a new feeling for me. Unfortunately the longer this process goes on, the angrier I get. When I am really mad I start to think that if money was not a problem, my response to ANY offer from the school district would be to have our attorney tell the district that the offer is absolutely unacceptable—and we will be going the whole way to try and seek justice.

Unfortunately, money is an issue and reality sets in quickly.

We have spent thousands of dollars on private interventions, appropriate schooling, and attorney fees to date. And the well is running dry, so to speak. Our son is entitled by law to a free and appropriate education.

Because of our work ethic, we were able to save up enough to pay for all these services. However, our dreams of being able to put money away for Kyle and Liam's college tuition, and make home improvements, came to a halt during this fight for justice.

You know how it is. You work as hard as you can, and sometimes, it is just not enough. But you can't stop. You have to keep going.

Like so many families, as soon as our paychecks come, they are gone to pay various people and bills.

The process slowly moved along, and as we prepared for our hearing, the school provided another offer. Not a significant offer, but a small amount of money for years of pain.

Our attorney advised us that there has been another offer, but she does not think it is significant. Her advice was to think it over carefully and get back to her.

Here we go again. The offer is not reasonable and not acceptable, and we countered.

We were told that we would hear back from the school district during a specific time frame. The time frame comes and goes, and we're still waiting to hear back.

So what did I do?

I started to review the testing results and prepare for our BSEA Hearing (if we do not agree on something reasonable). As a parent advocate, I start typing an important summary of Kyle's first neuropsychological testing to my attorney. It goes like this:

(Note: Some of the information concerning this testing has been omitted to protect my son's confidentiality. It is also important to document that Kyle has an average-to-very superior intelligence level as indicated in the neuropsychological I.Q. Tests.)

*Margaret, Attorney at Law*
*February 21, 1996*

*Dear Margaret,*

*As you are aware, the report that Ms. Chase, Ph.D., wrote is quite comprehensive; however, it is my opinion that there are vital parts of the report which need to be presented.*

*Below is a brief summary, which was not easy to document due to the fact that the report was 42 pages long and consisted of a neuropsychological evaluation, educational assessments and language assessments.*

• *"Kyle reported to this examiner that he experienced difficulties in his 'brain' when he struggled on school tasks and concerns about getting "in trouble" because of his difficulties."*

• *"Kyle openly complained of physical reactions he experienced in his 'brain' that seemed related to overload."*

• *"There were indications that many of his issues were related to negative experiences that he encountered. .............he did show some indications of anxiety."*

• *"He portrayed his home situation as nurturing, supportive and safe."*

• *"He reported some concerns about his difficulty in attending school..."*

- *"Kyle experiences problems with self-image that are related to inadequacies he experienced, and he is concerned with the impact of school learning and the reaction of others."*

- *"Everyday encounters were associated with negative feelings and stress..."*

- *"Within his educational program, he requires support from adults who are understanding of his profile and knowledgeable of the kind of assistance necessary for him to succeed, commensurate with his capabilities."*

- *"Kyle's pattern was significant for a learning disorder in many areas of reading."*

- *"His deficits greatly impede him from mastering the demands of a regular classroom program, and he does not demonstrate skills necessary for effective progress in written expression in a typical educational program, consistent with a learning disability in written expression that requires Special Education services."*

- *"On contextual reading and writing, performance was remarkable for functioning at the pre-school level, on reading passages and written expression, and his overall profile was consistent with the dyslexia as defined by the IDA (International Dyslexia Association)."*

- *"He requires intensive remediation for basic literacy and language skills, within programming that is individualized and paced for his particular needs and provided by specialists who understand the nature of his problems and his requirements for assistance."*

*It is my belief that it is extremely important to convey Kyle's learning disabilities to the BSEA Hearings Officer in a succinct format. Thank you for reading and considering this important input.*

*Sincerely,*

*Mary Jean Hughes, Ed.D.*

Please note that Ms. Ellen, Ph.D., the second independent neuropsychologist to evaluate my son Kyle, also expressed in writing the extent of my son Kyle's learning disabilities. However, she will be a witness at hearing, so I did not summarize her findings in this letter to my attorney. And so I end my letter to my attorney, and I feel a little better once it is written and sent.

It is now the spring of 1996.

Kyle is in the middle of third grade, and this process is in full swing (or at least, at this point, I hope it is the beginning of the end of this two-year process).

And what do you know? Once again, I begin to feel overwhelmed, and my car starts to fall apart...again!

How am I supposed to afford a private school tuition bill, a mortgage, attorney fees, and a new car payment?

Anyway, I keep reminding myself that we are not here for a long time, but a good time. My brother-in-law told me this saying, and he also has dyslexia. I often think about what a great saying and outlook he has.

So I guess the bills will keep coming, but since we all have our health and family, I feel like I cannot ask for more. In the grand scheme of things, I feel fortunate to have my son with me, and attending The Carroll School. As far as the car, we will deal with that somehow, some way.

It is still amazing to me after seeing all the injustices in the world that I take them so personally, and feel them, especially in my son's case, so viscerally.

What happens to the little boy or little girl who has dyslexia and has no parent? Or just one parent? Or parents who are not educated about dyslexia? Or who do not have the money to fight the bureaucracy?

Thinking of these children makes me sad. There has to be a better way. As my late mother, who was a wonderful educational advocate, said many times, there is a law for the rich and a law for the poor. If any reader has the financial means to donate to the International Dyslexia Association, it may help a struggling child who is not as fortunate as Kyle. The address of this wonderful organization is in the Author's Notes.

My late mother would be incredibly proud of her grandson Kyle, and would have loved to be at his Special Visitor Days at his new school. She was a parent who intuitively knew what her children with learning differences needed, whether it be one-on-one tutors, extra time to complete projects or vision therapy back in the early 1970s—which is quite remarkable. My late mother is at peace and is always with us in spirit.

Although there are much greater injustices in the world, the refusal to appropriately educate our children with learning disabilities is one that should not be overlooked. This is an important case, which affects a young boy, his school career and his entire family. My late parents and two great people in my life currently, Moe and Hunna Gillen, have taught and encouraged me to seek justice for Kyle.

Well, it is more than two years later from when this process all started, and our attorney has set up some meetings with Kyle's reading tutor and his second grade teacher—who retired after 20 years of teaching at the private school he attends.

Yes, we are moving forward, but I can't stop thinking, "Where would Kyle be educationally, socially, and emotionally if he was left in an educational system that steadfastly refused him the appropriate educational interventions he needs—and that he is entitled to?"

What a scary thought!

So I think more about how I can continue to advocate for my son—and off I go, writing another letter to send to my attorney. As the reader can tell, when I take pencil to paper or start typing an important letter, I take it seriously as part of my parent advocacy role.

My goal in writing the following letter is to assist my attorney with advocating for Kyle in any way I am able. By quoting a Supreme Court Justice, it is my hope that anyone who respects the laws of our country, and who wants to see justice done for every disabled child, will be inspired. This letter goes like this:

*Margaret, Attorney at Law*
*March 21, 1996*

*Dear Margaret,*

*My sister sent me some information on the Advisory on Jones vs. Smith, the U.S. Supreme Court Decision on Burden of Proof in Special Education Appeal Cases. According to the Commissioner of Education in Massachusetts, "The Jones decision will have little if any impact in our state, since attorneys and advocates for parents and school districts generally have assumed that the party initiating a Special Education appeal bears the burden of proof, and they have prepared and presented their cases accordingly. The U. S. Supreme*

*Court has now affirmed this rule under the Individuals with Disabilities Education Act (IDEA)."*

*However, I found it interesting reading some of the Supreme Court's decision. I have attached the following points, which I think relate to Kyle's case. I'm not a lawyer but I have the utmost respect for this field due to the complexities. Anyway, my perception is that Kyle is entitled to an Individualized Educational Plan (IEP) due to his disabilities, based on the law. There is no question in my mind, and I feel as though a fair person will understand that Kyle is entitled to an IEP and a free and appropriate education.*

*I can only conclude that our public schools personnel did not facilitate or participate in a cooperative process between us as Kyle's parents and themselves (the school personnel), and as Justice O'Connor observed "that the core of the statute is the cooperative process that it established between parents and schools." We, on the other hand, tried over and over again to collaborate and facilitate participation in a cooperative process.*

*Based on the many memoranda and meetings I wrote or participated in with the principal, head of Special Education and superintendent in our home town, it felt as though I was always attempting in person to facilitate participation in a cooperative process or articulate one in writing.*

*I understand differences of opinion, and respect them a great deal. But in the face of such overwhelming evidence, I do not understand what, in my opinion, was either negligence in not giving such a deserving child an IEP or the result of a clearly conflicted decision making process.*

*Kyle still struggles with school to this very moment, but he is in an appropriate environment. As a parent, all that I can do is to follow the process and keep him learning in the way his intellectual profile will allow him to.*

*Children with dyslexia typically experience greater difficulty with executive function, which includes attention processes, self-regulation, goal setting, initiating, and inhibiting behavior. Some behavior and social problems observed in children with dyslexia are related to poor executive functioning. They often also have problems with organization, planning, prioritizing, analyzing tasks, and completing a sequence of activities. Cognitive impairments can include memory problems, slowed information processing and language disturbances. Unfortunately, Kyle experiences all of the above.*

*Students with dyslexia are eligible for services under the Individuals with Disabilities Education Act (IDEA). To receive services, the learning disabilities must adversely affect students' educational performances and students require specialized instruction. Children such as Kyle require specialized instruction in order to make effective progress. The proposed 504 Plan would not have been appropriate to meet Kyle's learning needs.*

*Special Education programs are frequently selected as intervention of choice for students with dyslexia because they can provide a lower adult-pupil ratio, individually designed curriculum and specialized instruction, and necessary therapies.*

*Empirically supported teaching strategies such as using the Orton Gillingham (OG) method are effective with students who have dyslexia. The unique neurological profile of my son Kyle proves he is in need of specialized instruction. His greatest difficulties at this time relate to his auditory discrimination/auditory processing, reading comprehension, organization and his writing; however, he struggles in other areas as well.*

*Margaret, as Justice O'Connor put in writing in her decision "Under IDEA, school districts must create an individualized education program for each disabled child." As you are aware the public schools failed to do so even though the data was clear Kyle was disabled and in need of an IEP. We made several good faith attempts to create a cooperative process with no success.*

*Sorry for all the emails and letters, but "education is power." Thanks for reading this. I hope this information helps as we prepare to go to hearing and seek justice.*

*Sincerely,*

*Mary Jean Hughes, Ed.D.*

Well, another letter is written to Margaret, my attorney, and I feel a little better after it is sent. The process is moving slowly but surely.

But it is too long from when my son should have been deemed eligible for an IEP, and I am still waiting for justice.

As I stated, dyslexia is persistent. It does not go away. The stress is building, as it has been for way too long. Every time I try to convince myself that everything will be alright and will work out, I can't seem to really believe it because of the financial and emotional burden.

Suddenly, we get a call from our Special Education attorney, Margaret. She informs us there will be a Resolution Conference that will try and resolve the issue one last time prior to hearing, which is scheduled the following week.

## Resolution Conference

We arrived early, and my attorney Margaret, who knows me all too well, asked me "Mary Jean, what do you have in front of you?"

I informed her, "I have pictures of my son Kyle, because he is not a statistic or a monetary chip of any sort. He is a wonderful, bright, artistic young boy who has significant learning disabilities and deserves an appropriate education. I also brought some of Kyle's art work and pictures of structures he has built to show off his talents."

She just smiled, and we proceeded into the Resolution Conference.

Following the others, we walked into the room, and everyone seemed uptight. It was set up this way. The parents, and parents' attorney, Margaret, sat across from Mr. Grady, head of Special Education, and the school district's attorney. The mediator sat at the head of the table, and we began another tense meeting.

Although this meeting was long awaited, it was difficult to bear.

Finally, we did reach a settlement agreement, partly because at this point, we were emotionally and financially spent.

During this time, all I kept thinking about was writing a book to help others caught in these tense situations. As a matter of fact, at one point during our negotiations I said, "Margaret, by signing this agreement, it does NOT prohibit me from writing a book. Correct?" My attorney answered, "Correct."

The fact that a settlement agreement was finally reached gives me satisfaction as a parent; however, the journey to get to this point was agonizing, and in my opinion should not have been so difficult.

When I began this process, I never thought I would be going through all of this—much less standing up in front of so many people, and having to state my case.

But if I can do it, anyone can. You have to believe in yourself, and believe that you can handle anything they make you go through.

For all of that, our settlement agreement is more of a beginning than an end, because Kyle is so young, and his education has really only just begun.

And if anyone believes that I will stop before I get full and complete justice for my son Kyle, well, all I can say is, think again!

To be sure, should my future educational endeavors be as interesting as my past ones, I won't hesitate to put pen to paper again. I will do everything humanly possible to make sure my son's legal rights are protected, and that he receives an appropriate education based on the law.

Only next time, I will be more experienced!

As my late mother often said, "There is no better teacher than life itself."

With all that said, we are still struggling every day as a family living with dyslexia.

My dyslexia seems to have become more troublesome than ever before. Knowledge is great, but ignorance is bliss, as the saying goes. Kyle did share with me last night, after he finished his homework, that he likes doing homework with me because I understand dyslexia because I have it.

Although dyslexia is difficult, there are certainly worse challenges people face every day. We are blessed to have each other and our physical health.

In any event, this book is not all about my son and me. It is also about the American public school system's lack of insight into a very serious problem that is facing approximately 10 million of our children. It is well past the time to think creatively and help educators learn about scientifically proven teaching methods, and the importance of smaller class sizes to assist with this problem.

Many children with dyslexia end up with significant emotional problems due to their needs not being addressed in an appropriate fashion. Acting out and problems with the law also are often associated with feeling stupid or not smart.

Just think how much time our children spend in school. They spend six hours a day, five days a week for 180 days a year.

Then, multiply this number by 12 years. This is a significant amount for any child, teenager and adolescent, especially when they are in an environment that does not understand the complexities of this neurological problem.

However, these problems are not impossible to solve. It will take lots of time, effort and money. It will also take innovative ideas and action plans. With the correct composition of people and financial support, greater curriculums and teaching practices can occur.

These actions will benefit students like our son, and society as a whole. We live in the richest country in the world, and our society functions on the belief that if you work hard enough, anything is possible.

Moreover, the reality of today's global economy is that education is more important today than ever before.

As citizens, we must demand that our politicians stop "building bridges to nowhere" and finally once and for all fully fund legislation such as the No Child Left Behind (NCLB) Act.

Education is truly our bridge to a growing economy, and a productive society.

# Family Photo Album

This is Kyle at 8 months with my mother on St. Patrick's Day. My mother was born in Galway, Ireland, in 1924.

# Good Brothers &
# Good Friends

# Kyle's Strong Family Support System

To unc. Steve                    3/3/07 Kyle

Artist: Kyle, Age 10

Artist: Kyle, Age 10

# Summary

"I just barely got through school.
The problem was a learning disability,
at a time when there was nowhere to get help."

**Bruce Jenner,** Olympic gold medalist

# Summary

America deserves to provide the best for its citizens. We live in a country with vast resources and great opportunities. Everyone has the right to life, liberty and the pursuit of happiness.

As a parent and a concerned citizen, I want to try and make a difference. I want to tell my story in the hopes that I will make a change. Maybe I'll help parents identify their children as having dyslexia, so they can get the early intervention they need.

Or perhaps a principal will read this, and be motivated to change the way his or her school provides reading instruction.

Or perhaps a child or adolescent will read this, and realize he or she can do anything they put their mind to.

It was not easy for me to get a Doctorate in Education. (Or a Master's Degree, or a Bachelor's Degree for that matter, but you know what? I did it!)

People can take a great deal from you, but they can never take away your educational degrees or pursuits.

Make no mistake about it, education opens up doors. As a parent, that is what you want for your children— opportunities.

I hope Kyle learns that he is capable of doing whatever he wants. He may never go on to college, or he may go to Harvard. We don't have a crystal ball; we only have love and support in our hearts. As a parent, that is what I try and do every day. I simply love and support my two sons. If I do these two things well, I am accomplishing my biggest responsibilities.

When I lost my mother, it was the worst day of my life, but I know she is at peace and would be quite proud of her grandsons Kyle and Liam. She was a very spiritual person, and on the day she died we read from her daily word, which is a collection of a person's favorite prayers. My mother enjoyed these prayers immensely.

The prayer for that day speaks volumes. It goes like this:

*The grace of God is unconditional*
*love and acceptance.*

*We love our children and want what is best for*
*them not because of anything they have done,*
*but because they are miracles of life. Their very existence*
*makes them worthy of the best that we can provide.*

*Perhaps even more amazing is the unconditional*
*love our children give to us.*

*We may not be the best of parents in every moment of life, but we are doing the best we can. Children seem to instinctively know this.*

*As God's beloved children, we are all worthy of unconditional love and acceptance—the grace of God in action. No matter what our backgrounds or experiences, we are worthy of being treated with dignity and reverence.*

*Though we are unique individuals, we are also united by grace, which is God's gift to all.*

*By the grace of God I am what I am, and His grace towards me has not been in vain.*

**1 Corinthians** 15:10

What a wonderful prayer. Reading, although difficult for me, has offered me great pleasure at times.

Another wonderful writing by Hiam Ginott, who is a child psychologist and writer, goes like this:

I have come to the frightening conclusion. It is my personal approach that creates the climate. It is my daily mood that makes the weather. As a teacher, I possess tremendous power

to make a child's life miserable or
joyous. I can be a tool of torture or
an instrument of inspiration. I can
humiliate or humor, hurt or heal. In all
situations, it is my response that decides
whether a crisis will be escalated or
de-escalated, and a child humanized
or de-humanized.

Hiam Ginott

This prayer and this writing speak volumes about children and how they should be valued. Educators must recognize the power—the impact—their actions, or lack thereof, have on a child. For example, Kyle is now in fourth grade, and after receiving a positive report from his current teacher at his private school, he asked, "Did Ms. Connors (his first grade public school teacher) say I was bad?"

I tried to reassure him that Ms. Connors also knew he worked very hard. The reality is this. Kyle's first grade experience still haunts him three years later—and it is striking. That first grade year still, at times, weighs heavily on his mind.

The reason I documented these writings is that they have brought some comfort to me, and perhaps they will offer support to those out there reading this book.

Kyle continues to enjoy his school, and he has made amazing progress. He still understands that he has difficulty with some academic tasks, and school is not easy.

In fact, it is very difficult for Kyle. However, he knows he is in a safe environment and he is learning. He said to me one morning in the middle of fourth grade, "Sometimes what happens to me is when I am writing, I forget to write a letter or I write the same letter two times when I am not supposed to."

I told him he is a great student and how proud I am of him. Another day he jumped in the car and made a great sigh. When questioned if he was O.K., his response was, "It is not easy being dyslexic." I agree.

I have learned so much about dyslexia in the past few years. Parents should be aware that dyslexia impacts hearing, speaking, reading and writing. Some people view dyslexia as a reading disability alone. Although it is a reading disability, it is also a processing disability.

The best advice I have is this: "Do not let your child's disability take the heart and soul out of you."

This is, of course, much easier said than done. Focus on the positives. Enjoy and empower your child every day. If necessary, get help and support for yourself so you can be the best parent for your son or daughter.

I know that as a parent, placing Kyle at The Carroll School was the best decision for my son.

In fact, it was the only decision that could be made because all of the testing indicated Kyle had significant learning disabilities.

Kyle is thriving and loving the fourth grade. There is nothing more comforting than knowing that your child is being taught in a manner where he or she can continue to learn and grow as a person.

I have thanked God numerous times for creating such a fantastic school, which values education and services children with dyslexia. Kyle's desire to learn was almost extinguished by the end of first grade. Can you imagine?

I still can't believe this is real. It is unconscionable that educators would not give an IEP to such a deserving child. In my opinion, this is a gross injustice!

In fact, Kyle recently said to me that his friend was out sick from his fourth grade class, and he thought his friend had pneumonia. I said, "Kyle do you remember in first grade when you had pneumonia?" His response was striking!

Kyle said, "I would be sick any time I could to get out of first grade. It was so hard Mommy, why didn't I just quit?"

It is encouraging to note that I have not heard comments, like the ones below, from my son since he began at an appropriate school that teaches students with dyslexia:

"I hate school. I hate homework. How many more days are left in the school week? Who invented school anyway? I hate school, because it is hard and my brain gets mixed up. I'm too tired to do homework."

O.K., I'll admit I do occasionally still get complaints about school and the homework expectations from Kyle—but nothing compared to what we used to have to go through.

We both were exhausted by the end of Kyle's first grade year!

What a relief as a parent to have him in one of the most wonderful schools for language-based learning disabilities in the country, The Carroll School. Kyle still struggles with school and his dyslexia—and probably always will. The great part of this story is that he attends The Carroll School, which is unique and understands learning disabilities.

Because the purpose of this book is to assist struggling students and parents, I would suggest you complete the following if you believe your son or daughter has dyslexia:

## Early Interventions

- Speech and language therapy
- Occupational therapy
- Physical therapy (if necessary)
- Vision therapy
- **Independent Testing!**
- One-on-one specialized reading instruction/ tutoring
- Specialized instruction with an Individualized Educational Plan (IEP)
- Appropriate school environment
- Keep written logs about meetings with teachers, Special Education instructors, and anyone on your child's IEP team.
- Document phone conversations with dates and times.
- If you're able, hire an experienced educational advocate and Special Education attorney.
- Be Polite (Not always easy!)
- **Advocate, Advocate, and Advocate Some More**
- Join your local PAC.
- Familiarize yourself with the laws and your obligations.

As a parent, when you are advocating for your child, you feel as though you are an active participant—even when it feels like the public school Special Education team is ostracizing you.

Moreover, even when you have a great independent team, you must realize that you, as the parent, are the most important member of the team. It does not matter what "dream team" you have.

Who cares more about their child than a concerned parent?

Again, the part that saddens this author is the child who does not have the concerned parent, teacher or significant person in their life. Where do they end up? How do they succeed? There has to be a better way to monitor the American public education system.

There has to be more money allotted to allow the Special Education teams to do their jobs and provide the appropriate services to disabled students. Where does the money go? Who accounts for the money?

Maybe if parents of disabled children knew that they had the ability to raise funds to go directly to Special Education departments, they would do so. It is amazing what people have the ability to do when they put their mind to it.

The events in this book will hopefully open the eyes of many—as well as provide energy for creative problem solving; empower parents, teachers, administrators, therapists and all others who truly care about the well being of our children; and help, in some small way, to make a difference.

As I was always taught, there is power in numbers, so if people unite for the cause, maybe they can cause change for the better.

Certainly as a parent, I want to help facilitate change in a positive fashion for those children who struggle with language-based learning disabilities. I hope that this book has assisted with that goal.

I believe it is abundantly clear that the process, as it exists today, is stacked against the individual student and his or her parents who are challenging the system.

The primary reason is cost. It is virtually prohibitively expensive to hire neuropsychologists, educational advocates, tutors, lawyers, etc.

How can the average Joe and Jane navigate the system if they don't have the money, the educational training and knowledge of what their child's legal rights are to an appropriate education?

For all the "Joes and Janes" out there who need additional supports and resources, please see the Author's

Notes at the end of this book. Hopefully, you will be encouraged to seek justice for your child in any way possible.

Interestingly, when I was reviewing some school records that related to my own reading levels, I came across the following letter written to my parents when I was in the seventh grade.

It goes like this:

"A review of achievement test scores indicates that Mary Jean is not reading at a level consistent with her grade placement. Usually a youngster who appears to be experiencing difficulty in reading is assigned to the school's reading center for several hours of instruction per week."

Please note this pattern—and be the first one standing in line for help if there is a family history of learning disabilities.

One might say I have been an overachiever. The truth is I had a recurring nightmare that I would not graduate from the prestigious university I attended as an undergraduate

But I did.

Another roadblock came when one of my dissertation committee members doubted if I would ever complete the research and writing of my doctoral dissertation.

I took his comments, and like many people who have dyslexia, I refocused my efforts and with perseverance and with assistance of supportive people around me, I reached my goal. I have found that if people tell me I cannot do something, I am motivated to work harder and reach my goal.

This ability to persevere is found in many people who have dyslexia, simply because their neurological profile demands it of them. People who have dyslexia find the compensatory strategies they need to be very successful with perseverance, the correct people and appropriate environments.

We would be remiss not to mention how blessed we are to have worked with caring professionals such as Kyle's 1:1 reading tutor, his teachers at The Carroll School, our educational advocate, our fabulous Special Education attorney, and of course, our loving and supportive families.

# Epilogue

"I had to train myself to focus my attention.
I became very visual and learned how to create mental
images in order to comprehend what I read."

**Tom Cruise,** actor

# Epilogue

Recently, an article appeared in the Boston Globe about the high costs of Special Education. The title was "Special Needs a Costly Debate". The article concerned the rising expenses of Special Education. The average spending per student in Massachusetts in FY 2005 was $14,643 for Special Education and $7,421 for regular education.

There are two sides to this debate. Parent and advocate Trish Orlovsky said that school officials, "Hope parents aren't savvy enough to realize they are entitled to certain services." Another parent, Wilhelmina Howell, stated, "A lot of parents have to fight for everything they get."

On the other side of the argument, administrators point out with frustration that federal funding has never approached the level pledged when the national Special Education law was passed in 1975.

So where is the outrage?

This is the question I sit and ponder. If the administrators are frustrated that funding is such a big issue, then why not try and do something about it instead of focusing on fighting parents?

And should we simply accept that it is cheaper to pass children along in school, and wish them luck, as professor and attorney Andrew S. McAleer queries in his foreword to this book?

Or is it time to change the way society views dyslexia in order to obtain adequate funding and services?

In Kyle's case, I felt as though I was first advocating— trying to be cooperative and collaborative in assisting professionals within the school district to understand my son's need for an IEP and Special Education.

After these efforts went nowhere, I tried presenting pertinent evidence relating to his learning disability. When this failed, I began to realize that I was fighting a losing battle.

The description a person recently described so vividly and articulately seemed to fit my situation perfectly.

I was fighting the proverbial 800-pound gorilla. And this was exactly what it felt like.

Fortunately, Kyle is about to finish his third year at The Carroll School, and he is doing great! He has learned so many beneficial strategies to assist him, and he continues to develop and loves to learn.

At the young age of 10, he realizes he is in the appropriate learning environment and articulates his inspirations to continue to explore all of the vast opportunities he has in front of him. It is my belief, and Kyle's, that he will continue to thrive.

I also believe that if parents and educators work together, and review and embrace the research by Dr. Sally Shaywitz at Yale University, Professor Tami Katzir at Harvard University—and review the possible advantages of dyslexia rather than wallow in the public stigmas and overwhelming costs—perhaps vast opportunities will develop.

Moreover, perhaps effective strategies to raise monies to conquer this 800-pound gorilla will occur—or perhaps the gorilla will shrink in size, or ideally, cease to exist.

Hence, a child does not have to fail, parents do not have to fight, and administrators do not have to be frustrated. In fact, school districts might even embrace the children with dyslexia talents in a productive fashion, such as having alternative assessments as a benchmark versus the standard MCAS.

As Emerson observed, "The most advanced nations are always those who navigate the most."

Alternatives need to be discovered, created and monitored to assist our country with being a leader in the world for such endeavors such as educating and embracing up to perhaps 40 percent of its population with dyslexia or dyslexic symptoms. Can we afford not to?

Imagine how many of these children and young adults might be saved from drugs, problems with the law—and the insecurity from being perhaps a high school drop out—with the appropriate interventions.

And imagine still, the wonderful worlds these children will ultimately navigate on behalf of humankind.

I know that I am where I am today because of my mother, and I hope Kyle always knows he can do anything he puts his mind to.

My final thought, which I will end this book with, is a quote from Dr. Shaywitz:

> "I strongly believe that behind the success of every disabled child is a passionately committed, intensely engaged, and totally empowered parent, usually but not always the child's mother."

Artist: Kyle, Age 9

# Author's Notes

## Literary Inspirations

Corinthians 15:10 Bible Gateway.com; written entry in the Daily Word on June 25, 1999.

Dyslexia Awareness and Resource Center (2007). Quotes from famous dyslexics.

Emerson, Ralph Waldo. *Civilization,* Chapter 2.

Ginott, Hiam Child Psychologist and Writer (1975). *Teacher and Child, A Book for Parents and Teachers.*

Marshal, Abigail (2007). Davis Dyslexia Association (DDAI) 1601 Bayshore Highway, Suite 260 Burlingame, CA 94010 Telephone Number 650-692-7141 "The goals of DDAI are to increase worldwide awareness of: the perceptual gifts, talents or potential for genius that accompany and give rise to dyslexia; effective methods for resolving and learning disability to dyslexia. (2007).

O'Connor, Sandra (former Chief Justice of The United States of America) Supreme Court collection SCHAFFER v. WEAST (04-698) 546 U.S. 49 (2005) 377 F. 3d 449, affirmed.

Olenchak & Reis (2003). A personal communication in August 2003 Olenchak & Reis 2001; www.thefreelibrary.com

Reiff, Henry (1997). *Exceeding Expectations, a Ground Breaking Study of Adults with Learning Differences.*

Schworm, Peter February 18, 2007. *Boston Globe* Boston, Massachusetts Special Needs a Costly Debate 2007, Page A-1.

Shaywitz, Sally M.D., (2004). *Overcoming Dyslexia: A New and Complete Science Based Program for Reading Problems at Any Level.*

# Author's Notes

(continued)

## Valued Resources

The Carroll School
25 Baker Bridge Road
Lincoln, MA 01773
Phone: 781-259-8342
Fax: 781-259-8852
Web: www.carrollschool.org

Landmark School
429 Hale Street
Prides Crossing, MA 01965
Phone: 978-236-3010
Fax: 978-927-7268
Web: www.landmarkschool.org

International Dyslexia Association (IDA)
40 York Road, 4th floor
Baltimore, MD 21204-5202 USA
Phone: 410-296-0232
Fax: 410-321-5069
Web: www.interdys.org

Masonic Learning Centers for Children, Inc.
33 Marrett Road
Lexington, MA 02421
Phone: 781-862-8518
Toll-Free Number: 877-861-0528
Fax: 781-862-4514
Web: www.childrenslearningcenters.org

The Federation of Children with Special Needs
1135 Tremont Street, Suite 420
Boston, MA 02120
Phone: 617-236-7210
Fax: 617-572-2094
Web: www.fcsn.org

---

**"Children with dyslexia often have a different view of the world. Isn't the world lucky they do?"**

Adopted from
**The Carroll School**

---

# Notes & Reminders

# Notes & Reminders

# Notes & Reminders

# Notes & Reminders

# Notes & Reminders

# Notes & Reminders